THE
ORIGIN OF THE STATE

BY

ROBERT H. LOWIE

PROFESSOR OF ANTHROPOLOGY
UNIVERSITY OF CALIFORNIA

NEW YORK
RUSSELL & RUSSELL · INC
1962

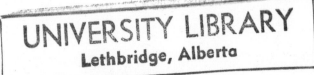
PRINTED IN THE UNITED STATES

PREFACE

The subject of government among the simpler peoples of the world was briefly treated in my book on *Primitive Society* (1920). However, at that time I was not yet acquainted with certain theoretical views, notably those of Professor Oppenheimer. In subsequent lectures at the University of California I attempted to supplement my earlier exposition, and a brief summary was published in *The Freeman* (July 19 and 26, 1922). To my surprise this virtually inaccessible essay is still referred to from time to time. Since the topic is one of perennial interest to students of sociology, political science, and comparative jurisprudence, it seemed worth while to issue the article in greatly expanded form. The ethnographical data presented will conceivably be useful to the outsider working in neighboring fields, especially as they very easily elude his notice.

In order to forestall misunderstandings, I premise that my interpretation of the relations of associations with the state has appreciably altered in this revised version.

Several friends have been good enough to read or listen to portions or all of the manuscript—

among them particularly Professor Leslie Spier of the University of Washington, Mr. Ronald Olson of the University of California, and Mr. Donald Clark. I take this opportunity to express my appreciation of their trouble and their kindly comments.

ROBERT H. LOWIE

UNIVERSITY OF CALIFORNIA
1927

CONTENTS

THE ORIGIN OF THE STATE

INTRODUCTION: THE PROBLEM

Are primitive peoples organized in a way that warrants our speaking of their governmental units as "states," or at least of rudiments of such? Everything naturally hinges on the sense attached to the term. It is easy to coin a definition that would give a monopoly of statehood to, say, the United States or Imperial Germany. We could similarly define "literature" so as to exclude the Homeric poems while they were merely recited and to include them after they were written down; and we might further decree that only compulsory monogamy was worthy of the name of "marriage." But such procedure, however etymologically or ethically justifiable, would wrest asunder what manifestly belongs together, thus defeating the purposes of scientific classification. Our initial query is thus seen to be typical of a genus, to wit: Have the simpler peoples psychological equivalents of the main cultural manifestations found in more complex societies? For example, if we accept Professor Maciver's commonsense characterization of our state,[1] we shall ask: Do illiterate peoples, too, maintain political order

[1] R. M. Maciver, *Community* (1924), 28-30.

1

within fixed territorial limits? Now, as will be seen later, it has been argued that they recognize no such limits and that they all manage somehow to survive in a condition of anarchy. Whether that is the correct view, remains to be determined by empirical inquiry; but on the analogy of corresponding comparisons we shall be inclined to reject it. As there was a literature before writing; as there are forms of the family that differ *toto coelo* from the modern ideal of permanent and obligatory monogamy; so there may be peoples with political ideals deviating widely from ours and with equally divergent processes for their maintenance. Professor Thurnwald has wisely warned us against assuming a supercilious egocentric position. Our modern state, he contends, is no more than one of many abstract possibilities and has varied in time. If we still designate as "states" countries willing to subordinate themselves to a League of Nations or to a Soviet council, we can hardly deny the title to governmental fabrics (*Herrschaftsgebilde*) of the illiterate peoples.[2] Similarly, the great historian of antiquity, Eduard Meyer, pleads for the absolute universality of the state in human society.[3]

With these and other scholars we shall endeavor to apply to primitive and civilized societies alike

[2] R. Thurnwald, *Die Gemeinde der Bânaro* (Stuttgart, 1921), 234.
[3] E. Meyer, *Geschichte des Altertums* (1907), I, *Erste Hälfte:* 10-12.

the principle of continuity and psychic unity and will attempt to bridge the gap between them by intermediate steps. In order to envisage the problem more clearly, let us begin by reconstructing as nearly as may be the primeval "state." For this purpose we are not merely thrown back upon *a priori* speculation. Though it is a commonplace of ethnology that peoples may advance very unevenly in different phases of civilization, features shared without exception by all unequivocally rudest tribes may be reasonably accepted as not only primitive but *primeval*. Fortunately, there is essential agreement as to what peoples are to be graded as lowest in the scale of complexity, there is virtual uniformity in the political features of these several tribes, and, finally, there is an exceptional harmony between these empirical findings and the conjectures of abstract reasoning. Accordingly, we may proceed with a confidence rare indeed in theoretical ethnology.

The tribes of simplest culture embrace the Tasmanians, the various Pygmy groups of the world, the Australians, the Tierra del Fuegians of southernmost South America, the Shoshoneans of Nevada, and various other tribes—all of them hunters, fishermen, and collectors of wild plants, ignorant of tillage, of stock breeding, and of metal work. Since the Pygmies of the Andaman Islands are perhaps the best known of these peoples, a brief summary of the relevant part of their culture seems desirable.

Although the Andamanese are often mentioned as if they were a homogeneous group, the supposed uniformity applies only to their racial characteristics. Professor Radcliffe-Brown recognizes ten tribes in the Great Andaman, and three in the Little Andaman group, each with linguistic and to some extent cultural peculiarities. The political unit, however, is still smaller. Every tribe consisted of approximately ten autonomous land-owning bands with distinctive hunting territories on which trespass was resented. Each of these minor groups embraced on the average from forty to fifty persons of all ages, the mean area being about 16 square miles. A typical encampment might consist of ten families in as many huts, with a few bachelors and unmarried women. There is no organized government, administration being regulated by the old men and women, to whom their juniors show marked respect. In addition to age, skill in hunting or warfare, liberality, and an even temper bestow prestige, and if men combine these desirable traits they come to rank as headmen, their opinion carries weight, and they are voluntarily aided by young henchmen. "In each local group there was usually to be found one man who thus by his influence could control and direct others." This headman, however, wielded no authority by virtue of his office, exerting his influence solely as a result of his personality. There was no formal penalty even for murder, except that anti-social behavior resulted in the loss of popular esteem—itself, however, a serious punishment for the Andaman Islander.[4]

To supplement these observations by data from two remote regions of the New World, the Paiute Shoshoneans of Utah and Nevada had a headman for the rabbit hunt, but apart from that occasion his authority was nil. For a considerable portion of the year an important part of this tribe, the Shivwits, would split up into distinct families, each claiming the right to a spring and the seeds growing near it; and it was only in the winter that they all united to form a single hunting band.[5] Similar conditions prevailed among the Yahgan of Tierra del Fuego. Their miniature communities normally lacked coercive agencies. Chiefs were lacking, and it was only at the time of their festivals that order was preserved by special officials—the master of ceremonies and a sort of constable to guard the sacred lodge against the approach of the uninitiated.[6]

It appears, then, that the primeval political unit

[4] A. R. Brown, *The Andaman Islanders* (1922), 13, 22–87.
[5] R. H. Lowie, *Notes on Shoshonean Ethnography,* in *Anthrop. Papers, Amer. Mus. Natural History* (1924), XX: 284.
[6] W. Koppers, *Unter Feuerland-Indianern* (1924), 53, 233.

was insignificant in numbers and habitat, and was necessarily constituted in large measure of blood kindred. Of differences in hereditary status no suggestion has been found. There were no political institutions or officials, but merely headmen enjoying purely personal authority. The groups nevertheless cohered through the unenforced acceptance of certain standards, violation of which precipitated general disapproval.

It must be admitted that this archaic pattern contrasts strangely with its equivalent in modern civilizations. Instead of a horde of fifty or a hundred folk, mostly related by blood or marriage, we find enormous aggregates of population scattered, it may be, over half a continent; frequently there are hereditary class differences; invariably there are individuals vested with authority and often asserting for the state which they serve or control that unconditional supremacy known as sovereignty. If the principle of continuity really holds for this compartment of culture, we must discover the processes that could convert a community of the Andamanese model into the elaborate structures of modern times.

I

THE SIZE OF THE STATE

Mere size is never a sound classificatory principle, hence no apology is needed for putting the diminutive groups mentioned above into the same category with the British Empire. If they otherwise conform to the concept of statehood, it would be inexcusable to exclude them on the ground of smallness. Empirically, to be sure, size may make a tremendous difference; but theoretically communities having a thousandth of the population of old Serbia may rank on a par with Russia and Austria-Hungary. From an anthropological point of view, however, it is interesting to inquire into the dynamics of aggrandizement; and here the New World—supplying, as it does, the whole gamut from the particularism of the Nevada Shoshoneans or typical Californians to the vast dominion of the Incas of Peru—provides suggestive material. We shall not, of course, naïvely assume that other continents must exactly parallel the conditions found in America.

Separatism could hardly go further than in the case of some of our Californian natives. As Professor A. L. Kroeber has often insisted,[1] the very

[1] *Handbook of California Indians* (1925), 8–15, 726–830.

term "tribe" is almost ludicrously inappropriate
when applied to many of the peoples in this area.
Census reports and estimates must not be allowed
to foster misconceptions on this point. Thus,
Kroeber sets the old Yurok population at 2,500;
while the Maidu are estimated at from 4,000 to
9,000 by Dixon and Kroeber, respectively. But
"Yurok" and "Maidu" in this context carries no
political connotation whatsoever, no more than the
term "Andamanese." Though the people of one
village were culturally indistinguishable from the
next, though their dialects might be mutually intelligible or even identical, there was no cohesion
of neighboring settlements, trespassers were kept
out by an elaborate sentry service and were sometimes summarily dispatched. The single settlement
of possibly a hundred souls, predominantly constituted of blood kin, stands out as the *only* political
unit. The suspicion directed towards all strangers
inevitably discouraged travel and precluded the
evolution of major groups.

However, it is not necessary to go further afield
than to the natives of the Colorado River region—
all of the Yuman family of languages—to encounter
a different condition of affairs. It is true that even
the Mohave, to cite a conspicuous example, probably
never exceeded 3,000. Yet, for one thing, this
figure, trifling enough from our point of view, is

enormous in contrast to the hundred or two hundred souls of a Yurok community. But still more important is the difference in outlook. The Yurok individual was rooted in a definite village, localization indeed going so far that even house sites bore distinctive names. In a group of adjacent settlements one member "was sometimes involved in a feud while another directly across the river looked on." Not so on the Colorado River. The Mohave "think . . . of themselves as a national entity, the *Hamakhava*. They think also of their land as a country, and of its numberless places. They do not think of its settlements. Where a man is born or lives is like the circumstance of a street number among ourselves, not part of the fabric of his career. The man stands in relation to the group as a whole, and this group owns a certain tract rich in associations; but the village does not enter into the scheme."[2]

The Mohave were not afraid of long journeys. They mingled freely among their fellows in other local divisions, and warlike enterprises carried them far to the west, even to the territory of the Chumash on the Pacific coast. Indeed, the Yumans went further in evolving not merely a national consciousness but even a tendency toward relatively stable alliances with alien groups, the Mohave and Yuma

[2] Kroeber, *Handbook*, 727.

being regularly united against the Maricopa and Cocopa.

At first blush we might be tempted to derive this development from the somewhat higher cultural status of the Colorado River tribes when compared to the Central Californians; for they share earthenware with other South Californians, and alone, among natives of this state, till the soil. A moment's reflection proves, however, that Yuman nationalism cannot be simply correlated with this advancement in material culture. The Pueblo Indians, such as the Hopi, far surpass the Yumans both as expert horticulturists and as potters; yet the centrifugal tendencies of their villages rival Central Californian separatism. Even the tiny hamlet of Shipaulovi, with a population of barely a hundred, jealously guards its individuality against neighboring villages.

With greater plausibility we can link Colorado River nationalism with the martial cast of Yuman culture. It is easy to understand that for the effective prosecution of hostilities greater numbers and greater coherence were required than existed in Yurok and Maidu villages. As an initial step toward widening of affiliations, this factor was probably a potent influence. On the other hand, its significance should not be overrated. It may indeed overcome the excessive provincialism of the Northern Californians, but it hardly suffices by

itself to lead beyond this modest stage of achievement. The military spirit may obviously act as a
disruptive force. The Polynesians were presumably
as warlike as any people, but everywhere we find
them rent into petty principalities by the jealousies
of bickering chiefs. This was by no means a con-
sequence of their insular restriction as to territory;
New Zealand offered ample space for the integrat-
ing hand of a great administrator, but formed no
exception to the rule. Even in Hawaii the sub-
jugation of diverse tiny domains under a common
rule was effected only a little over a century ago.

The same failure in major political organization characterized our ever-fighting Plains Indians.
Thus, the possible 4,000 Crow Indians of a hundred years ago were divided into two friendly but
politically independent sections, the River and the
Mountain Crow. Similarly, the Dakota, popularly
known as "Sioux," were far from forming a governmental unit. Even the Oglala section of the Teton
branch had four subdivisions, and when two of
them were placed under the Pine Ridge Agency
it was only in deference to the wishes of United
States officialdom that they merged their separate
schemes of government.[3] Thus, the most we can
say is that martial aspirations are probably incon-

[3] C. Wissler, *Societies and Ceremonial Associations in the Oglala Division of the Teton-Dakota* in *Anthrop. Papers, A.M.N.H.* (1912), XI: 7.

sistent with the extreme particularism of the Pacific coast.

On the other hand, where prowess in war was coupled with a sense for organization the results were striking. Thus, Creek towns were leagued together even in De Soto's day (1540); and the Creek confederacy, which in the eighteenth century embraced some fifty towns and six distinct languages, was able to hold Alabama and Georgia against the invasion of northern tribes. So the famous Iroquois league, reported to have been founded by Hiawatha about 1570, lorded it over an area extending from the Ottawa to the Tennessee and from the Kennebec to the Illinois and Lake Michigan.[4]

The famous Aztec "empire" was apparently reared on a similar foundation, that is, on the confederation of three tribes united to wrest tribute from their neighbors, one-fifth of the spoils going to Tlacopa, while the lion's share was evenly divided between Mexico and Tezcoco. Expert opinion will probably come to take an intermediate position between that of the early Spanish chroniclers and the extreme skepticism of L. H. Morgan and Adolphe Bandelier. That Mexico was a vast feudal monarchy on the medieval European model, is inherently improbable. On the other hand, Morgan's and

[4] F. W. Hodge, *Handbook of American Indians North of Mexico* (1907), I: 363, 618.

Bandelier's *a priori* argument that all American aborigines *must* have been democratic is absurd inasmuch as incontrovertible evidence from British Columbia and the Natchez of the lower Mississippi establishes marked class distinctions on a plane of culture far lower than the Mexican. Apparently what happened in Mexico was the following. Socially, the distinction that had originally been based on personal bravery was made hereditary, and when conquered lands were distributed among the warriors these definitely became a favored class. The Aztec war chief—elected, but from among a narrow circle of kin—"was probably well started on the road to becoming a king, but had not yet arrived." Furnished by Mexico to the league as a whole, he doubtless was able, under favorable conditions, to exert a considerable influence on the affairs of the realm and to integrate its constitution; and while the sphere of his power probably never extended beyond a quarter of a million people, this is a far cry from the Californian hamlets described above and brings the figure well within the range of variability of historic states.[5]

[5] L. H. Morgan, *Ancient Society* (1877), Part II, Chapter 7. A. Bandelier, in *Reports of the Peabody Museum* (1878), II: 385–448. P. Radin, *Sources and Authenticity of the History of the Ancient Mexicans,* in *Univ. Cal. Pub.* (1920), XVII: 132–150. T. T. Waterman, *Bandelier's Contribution to the Study of Ancient Mexican Social Organization (ibid.,* 1917), XII: 249–282. H. J. Spinden, *Ancient Civilizations of Mexico and Central America* (1917), 181–187.

In ancient Peru the severer organization of the Incas led to the establishment of a much larger area under central control. The empire comprised Peru, western Ecuador as far as Quito, a part of the Bolivian plateau, and the coast of Chile north of Rio Maule—probably even the Andean section of the Argentine, though it must be admitted that at the margins authority was merely nominal. Here, even more than in Mexico, the secret of expansion lay in military conquest, facilitated and strengthened by an elaborate governmental machinery. The conquered tribes, grouped in fours, were united under a governor of Inca lineage, who levied troops, collected tribute, supervised obligatory labors, and administered justice. He was expected to avert anti-Inca agitation and reported to the Inca ruler at an annual festival. All the subject tribes were grouped into four provinces, under ministers who resided not in these provinces but in Cuzco, the national capital. In order to maintain their dominion, the Incas maintained garrisons recruited from tribes alien to those among whom they were stationed. For economic or political reasons members of the various tribes might be deported to remote regions. The entire population was split up into age classes and obliged to work under the direction of Inca overseers.[6]

[6] H. Beuchat, *Manuel d'Archéologie américaine* (1912), 607; H. Cunow,

The American data, then, suggest that the ex-
igencies of warfare may have initiated the evolution of more extensive units, but the more closely
we examine the facts, the more clearly it appears
that an additional determinant was required for
effective larger aggregates. Rationalistic conceptions naturally dominate us nowadays to such an
extent that we find it difficult to envisage war from
any angle but that of industrial imperialism. Yet
the actual practices of many primitive tribes were
directly antithetical to such a view. Yurok law
demanded that in any ultimate settlement of differences each slain or injured person should be compensated for according to a fairly fixed standard,
seized property being restored and indemnities being
paid for what had been destroyed. There were no
captives taken, and the idea of tribute was wholly
foreign to the Yurok.[7] To pass to another region,
a typical Australian tribe was so intimately bound
up by sentimental and religious bonds with the
ancestral tract of land that no victorious group
ever dreamt of dispossessing the vanquished of their
territory. Similarly, in one of the Solomon Islands
the immigrant chiefs are actually landless, having
never thought of expropriating the original occu-

Die soziale Verfassung des Inkareichs (1896); Clements Markham,
History of Peru (1892), 35 seq.
[7] Kroeber, Handbook, 49.

pants.[8] Again, though there is positive evidence
that some of the Plains Indian tribes of North
America ousted others in search of new hunting
grounds—especially after the introduction of fire-
arms—the normal mode of waging hostilities involved no expropriation and only secondarily or
incidentally the winning of booty. They were es-
sentially playing at a game of chivalry in which the
individuals who followed the rules scored points of
honor. Their high regard for the lives of fellow
tribesmen readily led to the abandonment of warlike
operations when a handful had been slain and sometimes made a leader responsible for the loss of his
followers. That such notions did not favor growth
by conquest hardly requires proof. We must accordingly recognize with Dr. William C. Macleod [9]
the importance of ideological factors over and above
those of a rationalistic or specifically economic order.
It is not enough that one society should defeat another, just as it does not suffice for two societies to
share a language or to allow each other's members
to join in ceremonial activities. Such conditions
may be ancillary, but they are not adequate. What
is required is some centralizing authority powerful
enough to counteract primitive separatism. If the
legendary narratives of the Iroquois concerning

[8] R. H. Codrington, *The Melanesians* (1891), 50.
[9] *The Origin of the State* (1924).

Hiawatha may be accepted, union of distinct peoples may be effected through peaceful means by the sagacity of a far-seeing statesman. On the other hand, a more frequent method has certainly been the defeat of rival populations, *if followed by their incorporation in a common polity.* Upon this crucial point of organizing ability after conquest the possibility of permanent extension hinges. It was by this means that in 1796 Kamehameha came to bring under his sway the many petty rulers of the Hawaiian Islands.[10]

This combined effect of militarism and administrative aptitude, especially under the influence of a potent personality, is well exemplified by African history. It would be an error to suppose that the Sudanese and Bantu Negroes uniformly followed the political pattern of such vast monarchies as Uganda, where several million people were subject to a single sovereign. Though it is true that such cases were remarkably frequent in contrast to Oceanian and American particularism, the entire scale of magnitude found in America may be duplicated from Africa. Among the Pangwe, a Bantu tribe of southern Kamerun, Spanish Guinea, and the French Gaboon, *e.g.*, the political unit is the village with its two rows of houses and the men's assembly house, in which all public acts take place. There

[10] W. D. Alexander, *A Brief History of the Hawaiian People* (1899), 25 *seq.*

is no king nor even, in the strict sense, a chief, but
merely a headman, the wealthiest person in the
community, who is really devoid of authority.[11]
From this it is a far cry to the Xosa and other
Bantu of the southeast, with their constitutional
monarchs allied to a population of tens of thousands
by ties of sentiment which implied implicit obedience and pathetic loyalty on the one hand and on
the other a fond solicitude for the welfare of the
subjects. How a nation of impressive proportions
may be built on this foundation is illustrated by
the familiar history of the Zulu. Prior to about
1810 they were a petty group in no way superior
to the neighboring Kafir tribes. About the begin-
ning of the nineteenth century a prince named
Chaka, having quarreled with his father, fled to
Dingiswayo, the ruler of the Tetwa. Upon the
death of Chaka's father, Dingiswayo overthrew his
successor and put Chaka in his place, who thus was
a monarch by his patron's grace, but became independent on Dingiswayo's death. After some vi-
cissitudes of fortune Chaka became the dominant
figure in South African politics, conquering tribe
after tribe till his realm extended to Delagoa Bay,
embracing dozens of formerly independent tribes.
The steps by which this kingdom was founded were
the following. For one thing, Chaka was a military

[11] Günter Tessman, *Die Pangwe* (1913), I: 56; II: 262.

genius who revolutionized the traditional South Bantu tactics by substituting thrusting-spears for reed javelins and making his troops advance in serried ranks. Secondly, he perfected an idea already evolved by Dingiswayo, to wit, the maintenance of a standing army, variously estimated at from 12,000 to 50,000 and divided into regiments of 2,000 each. Above all, Chaka devised a method for incorporating the defeated peoples. Their chiefs were generally allowed to exercise authority as Chaka's deputies, except in so far as they might be superseded by royal favorites. The married men were sometimes killed off, but the bachelors were drafted into the army and women added to the King's harem. Some outlying groups were not actually brought within the fold but merely became tributaries, as in the case of the Thonga. The details of Chaka's reign, though of extraordinary interest, do not concern us here. His success was evidently due not merely to the warlike character of his people but to the capacity he exhibited for organizing both his fighting machine and the populations it subjected to his dominion.[12]

Without claiming that the examples here assembled hold universally, we may say that they render intelligible that progressive increase in size which has characterized the history of many states and indicate the initial stepping-stones in that development.

[12] Lowie, *Primitive Society* (1920), 373 *seq.*

II

CASTES

If we are to believe so keen a sociological writer as Professor Franz Oppenheimer,[1] the problem of the state is coterminous with that of caste. All the states known to history, he contends, are characterized by the domination of one class by another for the purpose of economic exploitation. It is indeed possible that these features may disappear in the future, but the change wrought thereby would be so fundamental as to render the old concept inapplicable and we should have to coin some new designation, such as *"Freibürgerschaft"* (free commonwealth) for the resulting type of civic organization. On the other hand, the simpler unstratified forms of society, represented, say, by the ruder hunting peoples and horticulturists of the globe illustrate, from Oppenheimer's point of view, merely anarchic antecedents of the state proper. For the Old World, at all events, Oppenheimer sketches the course of evolution in some detail. When pastoral nomads come into contact with a sedentary peasantry, they at first resort to the simple

[1] *Der Staat* (1907).

20

device of wholesale pillage and slaughter. Later,
however, an enlightened self-interest prompts them
to spare the victims, allowing them to gain their
livelihood and become objects of a more regular
and rational utilization. A fixed system of tribute
may arise, the tillers of the soil bringing their produce
to the herders' tents. Still later the nomads settle
in the peasants' territory, establishing military colo-
nies all over it, while granting to their subjects
a relative degree of independence in regard to their
internal affairs. Conceivably a representative of
the ruling class may fix his abode at each peasant
chief's residence. Finally, the two originally separate groups are welded into a national unit: the
martial overlords extort what they will from the
subordinate caste, but in turn protect them against
alien aggression. Community of speech aids in the
development of sentimental relations and the con-
sequent integration of the stratified whole, while
at the same time class consciousness is fostered by
the conquerors' myth of their native superiority.

This theory not only has a certain *a priori* plausibility but may be abundantly exemplified by facts.
In the light of our present knowledge even more
telling evidence can be presented than Oppenheimer
was able to glean from Ratzel's *Völkerkunde*, though
qualifications will have to be made as to interpretation. Let us examine some of these data.

In the Western Sudan there is a curiously stratified series of societies. The Mande and Fula are not merely divided into a patrician and a plebeian caste, but embrace a whole set of graded classes. The nobility—in consonance with the theory under discussion—comprises the pure-blooded conquerors of the country. At the opposite extreme are the blacksmiths, who are recruited from the unmixed aborigines—apparently of commoners' status. The native nobility, on the other hand, evolved into the minstrels' caste: they became the confidantes of the grandees of the realm, served as their patrons' eulogists, at times even browbeating them by their ability to rattle the family skeletons, and also acted as educators of noble youths. In addition to their mastery of song, they plied the trade of leather workers. Serfs were the offspring of liaisons between the overlords and native women; they were attached to the land, sometimes as many as a thousand being subject to a member of the ruling caste, but were themselves entitled to hold slaves and might be completely liberated through an appropriate formality. If we are to credit Frobenius, the aristocrats were descended from a warlike tribe of cattle breeders who overran and subjugated a horticultural people and subsequently evolved all the earmarks of caste, rivaling in pride and rigorous adherence to a conventional code the knights of

medieval Europe. The ideal patrician was hand-
some, liberal, and brave; he would never take an
unfair advantage of an opponent on the battlefield;
and while no gentleman might without loss of honor
steal property in plebeian fashion, cattle lifting on
a major scale was decidedly in his line; and he was
rather expected to befuddle himself with honey
beer or millet brew. In short, we might well say,
with reference to medieval Europe, "*Tout comme
chez nous.*" [2]

It is needless to point out the details cited that
fall in line with Oppenheimer's scheme. A curious
anomaly, however, challenges our attention. The
blacksmiths—the unalloyed aboriginal class—are not
"exploited," but on the contrary receive horticultural produce from the Mandingo; and we are explic-
itly told that they are not so much despised as feared.

That this phenomenon is not unique, appears
from the East African data, which supply us with a
veritable embarrassment of riches as regards material relevant to our theme. Thus, the Somali of
the East Horn have no less than three separate
pariah classes. One of these, however, the Yebir,
so far from being under the thumb of the dominant
population actually lives without work, in fact,
collects tribute from every Somali paterfamilias on

[2] L. Frobenius, *Kulturtypen aus dem Westsudan* (1910), 1-44. A.
Arcin, *La Guinée française* (1907), 257-276. L. Desplagnes, *Le Plateau
central nigérien* (1907), 167 *seq.*

the birth of a child, and from every bridegroom on his wedding day. This strange prerogative is based on the supposed supernatural powers of the Yebir, who are dreaded as sorcerers and charm makers,— also because it is said that they vanish without leaving a corpse behind when they die. Secondly, there are the Tomal or blacksmiths, upon whom the Somali depend for the manufacture of all knives, swords, spears, and hatchets. Finally, the Midgan serve as tanners and hunters. Every large family keeps a few of them as attendants, but they are held unclean so that marriage with them is tabooed, any transgressing Somali being degraded to the rank of a blacksmith.[3] The case of the Yebir evidently parallels that of the Sudanese blacksmiths and serves as a caution against applying an economic schematism to the social arrangements of primitive peoples. For under the spell of sentiment and of religious conceptions they, like other human beings, are likely to snap their fingers at utilitarian considerations.

The cattle-breeding Masai of British and what used to be German East Africa resemble the Somali in maintaining manifold relations with their several neighbors. The Bantu tillers surrounding them exemplify Oppenheimer's incipient stage for the evolution of a subject class: they form no part of

[3] R. E. Drake-Brockman, *British Somaliland* (1912), 210-220.

Masai polity at all, being merely exposed to sporadic
depredation and massacre at the hands of marauding Masai warriors. True to type, the stronger
people concocted ingenious rationalizations to justify
their conduct. God, it seems, gave the Masai all
the cattle in the world. If the wicked Bantu would
only peaceably yield their live stock, all unpleasant-
ness might be avoided. But alas! they impiously
cling to their possessions, and so spoliation becomes
a religious duty.

Rather different is the status of the Wandorobo,
who roam as hunters over Masai territory. They
are treated with contempt, but are utilized as spies.
Apart from such service, they are free from imposi-
tion of a specifically economic character for the simple
reason that the pastoral Masai, who have themselves completely abandoned the chase, will not eat
any game.

Finally, there is the pariah class of blacksmiths,
despised even by the Wandorobo. They were presumably at one time a separate tribe and, in consonance with this view, are beyond doubt primarily
an hereditary rather than an occupational group of
natives, no member being allowed to escape the
ignominy attached to his caste by ceasing to practice
the traditional art. On the other hand, in exceptional cases a Masai proper may act as a blacksmith
without definite loss of status, even though his

fellows will temporarily look askance at him. The blacksmiths live apart and are treated as a necessary evil, professional aptitude in no way mitigating an individual's position. No Masai stops at a blacksmith's encampment, or vice versa, and none would marry a blacksmith's daughter. The indispensable products of the pariahs' professional labors are treated as impure and before use must be liberated from defilement by application of grease. At night the very word for "smith" is tabooed lest its utterance cause lions to attack the camp. A Masai may with impunity slay a blacksmith, while even the accidental killing of a Masai by a pariah would have to be atoned for by the murder of several blacksmiths. Here, too, a farcical justification for the maltreatment of the weaker has been developed: God forbade bloodshed, and the blacksmiths by the weapons they manufacture invite men to transgress the divine commandment. The full ludicrousness of this rationalization is only brought home to us when we recall that the whole organization of the Masai hinges on the activities of their warriors' class and that kudos is almost wholly dependent on the slaughter of their enemies.[4]

While the Wandorobo and the blacksmiths still stand outside what may be called the Masai state, they evidently have a closer relationship to the

[4] M. Merker, *Die Masai* (1904), 110, 170, 196, 207, 246.

dominant people than do the Bantu, for through occupation of the same soil they represent an initial stage of union with their oppressors.

Perhaps even more instructive is the history of the "interlacustrine" region of East Africa framed by such landmarks as Victoria Nyanza, Lake Tanganyika and Lake Kivu. Here once more the clash of peoples distinct in lineage and occupation is the central phenomenon, and as usual the herders are almost everywhere in the ascendancy. Though sharing the Bantu speech of their victims, they commonly figure in the descriptive literature of the area as "Hamitic." As a suitable generic equivalent is not readily found, the term may be retained in this context. It must, however, be distinctly understood that these "Hamites" today do not speak a tongue related to that of the Galla of Abyssinia or of the ancient Egyptians; there is merely reasonable evidence that the speech of their ancestors would properly be classified as Hamitic. But whatever doubt may be voiced as to their ancient linguistic affiliations, in race the interlacustrine Hamites certainly stand out sharply from the peasantry of their habitat. While the latter are of moderate stature, stocky build, and generally Negroid type, the pastoral people attain extravagant tallness, coupled with slender proportions, and often suggest European physiognomies. The shortest man measured by Dr. Hans Meyer stood 5 ft. 10 inches, the majority of the male adults between 5 ft. 11 and 6 ft. 3, while a fair number ranged about and even considerably exceeded 6 ft. 7 inches. This racial trait is evidently of social significance since it serves to separate at a glance the main constituents of interlacustrine society.

As a typical sample of conditions in this area we may take the ancient kingdom of Unyoro, northwest of Lake Victoria Nyanza. The horticulturists are here definitely under the herders' thumbs. They bring grain to the district chiefs, who in turn pass on the bulk of this tribute to the King. But again cultural factors militate against a rational utilization of the subject class. Since the herdsmen have little use for a vegetable diet, disdain fish, and have taboos against most forms of wild game, the economic produce of their subjects holds slight interest for them. It is rather by exacting labor which they scorn as degrading to themselves, such as housebuilding and carrying of water or firewood, that the Hamites oppress the tillers of the soil. A breach of the taboos, *e.g.*, of that proscribing the mingling of milk and other food in a herdsman's stomach, is believed to be detrimental to the welfare of their beloved cattle, and this trivial superstition, from our point of view, sets a barrier to intensive exploitation of the subject tribe.

CASTES 29

Corresponding conditions hold sway in Ankole, east of Albert Lake, where the peasants "are the workers who do all the menial tasks for the pastoral clans, all the drudgery whether of transport, or of house and cattle kraal construction, in addition to supplying them with beer and any vegetable food they may require,"—such a diet being resorted to only in periods of stress.[5]

A special development has been reported from Ruanda and Urundi, the sections of the region adjoining Lake Kivu and the Belgian Congo.[6] Here we find not two, but three, racially and economically distinct groups: (1) the dominant pastoral Tussi, or Tutsi, Bantuized in speech but otherwise sharply separated from (2) the Hutu tillers of the soil and (3) the Twa hunters. The last mentioned are very short, though not, as was once supposed, genuine pygmies but rather a mixture of a moderately sized Negroid people with the Congolese pygmies.

The social and psychological interrelations of these castes are of the utmost suggestiveness. The Twa are clearly the lowest group, and the Hutu, let alone the Tussi, would never dream of intermarrying or contracting blood brotherhood with them. Nevertheless,

---

[5] J. Roscoe, *The Northern Bantu* (1915), 77–79, 103.
[6] Jan Czekanowski, *Forschungen im Nil-Kongo Zwischengebiet* (1917), I; also *Zeitschrift für Ethnologie* (1905), 591–615. R. Kandt, *Gewerbe in Ruanda*, in *Zeitschr. f. Ethnol.* (1904), 329. P. A. Arnoux, *Le Culte de la Société secrète des Imandwa au Ruanda*, in *Anthropos* (1912), 273–395, 529–558, 840–875; (1913) 110–134, 754–774.

the little folk view the Hutu peasants with contempt on account of their sedentary life and extend this feeling to their own renegade kin who have taken up a settled mode of existence and developed into professional potters. As the Hutu require more and more land for cultivation, they encroach upon the domain of the hunters when in need of new clearings, yet intruding peasants when not protected by weight of numbers are liable to be pillaged by the tiny forest dwellers. Notwithstanding this comparative independence with reference to the intermediate social class, the Twa acknowledge certain Hutu chiefs as their superiors and through them render tribute to the Tussi king.

Here, as in other sections of interlacustrine territory, class feeling rests upon, or is at least justified by differences in dietary regulations: the Tussi look down upon the Hutu for eating mutton and the flesh of goats, while both despise the Twa for indulging in poultry and eggs. But the superciliousness of the Tussi does not prevent their playing off the pariah caste against the peasants and in fact exhibiting some favoritism towards them. When a Tussi kills sheep sacrificially, he permits the Twa to gorge themselves with the flesh tabooed to himself; and certain of the less exalted official positions are reserved for the hunters. It is they who are privileged to carry the king on his travels, to

form his bodyguard, and to chant in royal processions; nay, oddly enough, in a population where
the upper class are frequently giants, the stunted
Twa act as executioners and as the police force.
That there are nevertheless rigidly drawn barriers to
the social promotion of a hunter, has already been
explained with reference to marriage and blood
brotherhood.

The position of the peasant class is rather different. Socially inferior they doubtless are, since
the Tussi scorn such useful occupations as tillage,
metallurgy, wood carving and arrow making, to all
of which the tillers are addicted; and at least with
the central districts of Ruanda the Hutu are a
down-trodden lot who must meekly submit without hope of redress when their land is destroyed by
the overlords' cattle. Yet for them, in contrast
to the Twa, the social lines are not drawn with
such inexorable rigor: an impoverished stock breeder
does not recoil from marrying a peasant woman; some
of the lower court offices are held by eminent Hutu;
and there is no law preventing blood brotherhood between peasant and herdsman.

Contrary to what might be assumed on the Masai
analogy, the superior status of the Tussi does not
rest on their martial character. Though numbering
barely 150,000 in a total population of 1,500,000,
they have succeeded in holding the two other classes

in subjection mainly by their political astuteness,—
by their own solidarity and their cleverness at
juggling existing conditions. They found the Hutu
split into an indefinite number of separatistic units,
each hereditary headman wielding little actual
authority, each tribelet pitted against its neighbors.
Profiting from this internecine warfare, the Tussi
readily conquered the country and altered existing
institutions by appointing the petty headman of
each group a royal official charged with the duties
of a taxgatherer. Thus, he came to be clothed with
real power, and henceforth it was to his interest to
champion the rulers' cause. Restive clans were
broken asunder and scattered among different chiefs
loyal to the King, their quasi feudal lord. The bulk
of the peasants cultivated the King's land and
worked for their immediate chief two or three
days a week. One group of them was organized
into a rustic aristocracy of landed braves exempt
from forced labor. An efficient police force kept
rigorous surveillance over the entire realm, spying
both on the paramount chiefs and on foreign visitors.

A peculiar and as yet somewhat enigmatic place
in Ruanda polity is occupied by the secret religious
society, which people joined in order to secure good
luck and social distinction. Strangely enough, admission occurs irrespective of both sex and caste,
though owing to the entrance fees few attain the

higher grades. The King, however, is excluded from the organization, royalty being represented by the Queen Dowager. It is nevertheless the King that appoints and deposes the head priest. A special set of functionaries assist the priest and together with the Twa form the royal bodyguard, act as bards and trumpeters, and lead criminals into exile. The higher degrees of the society carried with them various prerogatives, for example, that of bulldozing the populace at large into surrendering lavish supplies. Though the matter is far from clear, the admission of all three castes into this organization suggests an incipient integration of society lacking among the Masai, so that altogether the Ruanda institutions seem to provide still further evidence for Oppenheimer's thesis.

At this point we may conveniently halt in our survey of ethnographic information and inquire what precisely it demonstrates. The data certainly seem consonant with the scheme propounded by Oppenheimer and neatly illustrate several of its stages. Nevertheless, even for East Africa the interpretation offered has been summarily challenged by Dr. William Christie MacLeod. Arguing from the analogy of American conditions, this author calls for a critical revision of the evidence from the Dark Continent. While Oppenheimer accounts for social classes by conquest, MacLeod contends that such stratification would not result except where it was preceded by an aristocratic ideology among the conquerors.[7]

It may not be amiss here to indicate why anthropologists naturally have a certain bias in favor of Oppenheimer's view. So far as they are human, they cannot wholly divorce themselves from an interest in the *origins* of cultural phenomena. Now, while the "historical realists" among them see abundant evidence of human inventiveness in the adaptations made by man to varying environments, it is clear that the fund of original ideas is, after all, strictly limited and that man has no inexhaustible reservoir of originality to draw upon, that often enough the most desirable or, from our civilized point of view, obvious steps in advance *fail* to be made. From this angle the evolution of castes from a conflict of distinct tribes economizes thought on the problem of origins. We can readily understand how the mere conquest of one by another would lead to an hierarchical grading previously extant in neither, but the suggestion that the victors must already have had the notion of aristocracy prior to imposing it in the new situation they created by conquest presents an additional problem, *viz.*, how that ideology came into being. In so far

[7] *The Origin of the State, Reconsidered in the Light of the Data of Aboriginal North America* (Philadelphia, 1924), 39, 51, 90.

forth Oppenheimer's principle certainly simplifies the question.

However, this would not suffice to warrant acceptance in the face of valid counterarguments, and accordingly MacLeod's objections must be appraised on their merits. It should be noted first that his point of departure is the New World and that he questions the interpretation for Africa primarily because it does not seem to hold for America. Obviously the contention lacks cogency, for the developments need not be assumed to have been parallel in the two continents. More specifically, MacLeod discusses the case of Unyoro and suggests that the peasants did not form a numerous native group but were "very possibly immigrants who have entered the territory of the herding people in order to utilize the agricultural possibilities of the soil which were disdained by the herdsmen. The herdsmen seem to have been eager to have peasants enter their territories and raise grain." But this view runs counter to well established facts. Whatever may be the case in Unyoro, the tillers of such typical parts of the area as Ruanda and Urundi are far in excess of the herders and represent an older population subjected by the cattle rearing newcomers. It would be hyperskepticism to flout the unanimous testimony of half a dozen independent witnesses, especially when some of them take pains to show that the status of herders is less favorable in some regions, such as Uganda, than further south.

But this is far from accepting Oppenheimer's theory of the state. MacLeod certainly does well to direct attention to the prior polity of the conquering group. Are they really devoid of the criteria of statehood before subjugating the alien horticulturists? A fair consideration of the subject leads to a contrary conclusion. Both the Hutu and the Hamites evidently had some sort of governmental mechanism, and it is only by arbitrarily defining the state as an organization into castes that we can deny statehood to either. Oppenheimer's theory is, indeed, properly not a theory of the state at all but of hereditary social classes.

However, it cannot be regarded as adequately synthesizing even the phenomena of caste. For one thing, the German sociologist injects into the primitive atmosphere, charged with emotional values, the rationalism born of our industrial age. As Thurnwald has wisely remarked, nothing may be further from a primitive aristocracy than "the systematic, brutal, cynical exercise of economic power." Again and again we have seen how such exploitation is limited or even barred by purely ideological factors in the form of religious prejudice.[8]

---

[8] Thurnwald, "*Adel*" in *Reallexikon der Vorgeschichte* (1924), I: 18-21.

Finally, what Oppenheimer has shown is that castes have actually arisen through conquest; he has not proved that that is the only possible way they evolve. We must consider whether internal conditions could lead to social stratification; and it is assuredly a merit of MacLeod's treatise to have forcibly directed attention to this alternative. Without closely following his discussion we may single out for purposes of illustration the South Seas and the Pacific coast of North America.

In Oceania a mixture of racial types is generally assumed by students of physical anthropology, and the rigid division of society to be found there may in part be derived from such juxtaposition. But this is not the whole story. In Tonga, for example, gradations of rank are as conspicuous as anywhere. Yet Mr. E. W. Gifford tells me that the Tuitonga, the person of loftiest status, can be genealogically connected with a cook, the representative of the meanest occupation. Nor is it difficult to understand this on Tongan principles. The natives recognized a class of *egi*, noblemen, but the title went solely to the eldest son, all others sinking to the second degree of *matabule*. Similarly, the younger sons of the *matabule* became *mua*, and in corresponding fashion the younger sons of the *mua* were *tua*—the group embracing peasants and cooks. Thus, primogeniture, when consistently followed, inevitably creates differences in rank.

What applies to Tonga holds equally for New Zealand: at least, in part the distinctions of rank among the Maori are traceable to the principle of primogeniture. At the same time this and other Oceanian groups show that different factors need not be mutually exclusive. Slaves, as in many other parts of the world, were recruited from captives in war. From Fiji, indeed, Basil Thomson reports instances illustrative of Oppenheimer's theory—of the chief of a conquering people making himself king, his followers aristocrats, and the vanquished into commoners. In Fiji, however, the fortunes of war sometimes operated in a subtler manner. Fugitives from a neighboring tribe might seek settlement in a certain locality. Since the chief had the traditional prerogative of allotting waste lands for cultivation, both he and the newcomers would automatically acquire a new social character. Unlike the native peasants who were individual landowners, the aliens became definitely subordinate to the chief as their patron and personal overlord, to whom service and rent were due. And, retroactively, the existence of such a group of retainers was bound to enhance the chief's prestige and power.[9] It is clear from this example that we are dealing with

[9] Basil Thomson, *The Fijians* (1908), 59 f. and *passim*.

a plurality of factors, that even a military disaster
may create castes indirectly rather than through the
simple route plotted by the German sociologist.

Finally, a few words may be devoted to the best
known class system of North America, to wit, that
of the North Pacific coast. Tribes like the Nootka
of Vancouver Island follow the principle of primogeniture with results comparable to those noted for
Polynesia. Another parallel consists in the creation
of slaves through the capture of prisoners. But
the primary factor to be reckoned with has no
parallel in Polynesia, *viz.*, the emphasis placed on
corporeal and incorporeal wealth. In order fully
to enjoy the social birthright of a patrician, a chief
was expected to give frequent entertainments on a
lavish scale, for what conferred glory was the os-
tentatious display, nay, even the wanton destruction
rather than the hoarding of property. An ambitious
nobleman would not hesitate to burn up a big canoe
or to kill a slave for the sole purpose of impressing
the public with his affluence. But this strange
ideology was bound to bring into conflict the hereditary and the plutocratic principle. Though impoverished chiefs were long remembered as scions
of a noble line, commoners who had gained wealth
and emulated patrician example in its use—or
abuse—might rise to ascendancy, even though the
older families looked askance at such upstarts.

The following instructive episode of recent decades is told by the Kwakiutl. A commoner carried on a clandestine intrigue with a princess, who married him after her father's decease. The people at large were shocked. She bestowed upon her husband a chief's name and a "copper," *i.e.*, a piece of that metal corresponding to a bank note of high denomination, whereupon all men were sick at heart. Later a profligate woman lived in the upstart's house and bequeathed to him a copper valued at 700 blankets. In grandseigneurial fashion he now invited the people to a feast and assumed a new name. The people began calling him "chief" then, and he sat with the hereditary patricians. Later he tended an aged chief, who left him a third copper. Bloated with vanity, the *nouveau riche* sold it, invited all the Kwakiutl and bragged of not now being afraid of anyone. Three chiefs who felt themselves affronted by the boast conspired to effect his downfall and deliberately destroyed their coppers, worth 12,000, 9,000 and 18,000 blankets, respectively. The upstart, morally obliged to go them one better, failed to borrow the requisite 39,000 blankets and ignominiously relapsed into his original plebeian status.[10]

Though this story shows the ultimate triumph

[10] F. Boas, *Ethnology of the Kwakiutl* (Thirty-fourth Report, Bureau Amer. Ethnology 1921), 1110 *seq.*

of traditional prerogative over mere wealth, it also illustrates how potent this latter factor was even in recent times and what an influence it must have exerted in the incipient stages of the Northwest Coast system. Indeed, in a marginal outlier of the North Pacific culture zone, the Yurok of northwestern California, the foundation of caste is purely plutocratic. Even slaves are never recruited from prisoners in war but only from insolvent debtors. Characteristically enough, they were not as a rule killed for display, "the Yurok seeing no sense in the destruction of property." Apart from this class, social status depended on the actual property owned by an individual, and on the amount paid for his mother as her bride price. "Men of wealth made a point of paying large sums for their brides. They thereby enhanced their own standing and insured that of their children. . . . A bastard was one whose birth had never been properly paid for, and he stood at the bottom of the social scale." Such a one would not be permitted to enter the sweathouse, which otherwise served as a man's dormitory, workshop, and clubroom. The difference between rich and poor was linked with all those niceties typical of social stratification elsewhere, and the code of etiquette regulating a wealthy person's conduct was hardly less definite than a medieval knight's.[11]

[11] Kroeber, *Handbook of the Indians of California* (1925), 28, 29, 32, 80.

It is thus clear that MacLeod's *positive* contentions remain valid: internal conditions may suffice to create hereditary or approximately hereditary classes. But we need not therefore dispense with Oppenheimer's principle when purged of its doctrinaire elements. Apart from the concrete evidence on which it rests, it explains an African phenomenon otherwise not easily intelligible. For, contrary to what might be inferred from the facts expounded above, the natives of Africa are not as a whole a characteristically aristocratic people like the Polynesians. What confronts us again and again as we survey their forms of government from the Sudan to the Cape is not social classes but a tendency to autocracy: even in a vast country like Uganda, with a population of several millions, the chiefs subordinate to the king are emphatically not bluebloods. Dignitaries there are, and often, as among the Bakuba of the Congo, an amazing number and with an astonishing multiplicity of functions, but they are subject to a king who at least in theory is an absolute ruler [12] and in no sense constitute a patrician class. It is apparently only where, as in the Interlacustrine area, one people has vanquished another that a whole group appears hereditarily clothed with higher rank or doomed to a subordinate position.

[12] E. Torday and Joyce, *Les Bushongo* (1910), 53 *seq.*

III

SOVEREIGNTY

Sovereignty is the badge of the modern state. In Vinogradoff's words, the state "has assumed the monopoly of political coördination. It is the State which rules, makes laws and eventually enforces them by coercion. Such a State ... did not exist in ancient times. The commonwealth was not centered in one sovereign body towering immeasurably above single individuals and meting out to every one his portion of right. Therefore the necessary political elements which are never absent from any human society were distributed among formations which we regard now from the point of view of private law: churches, local bodies, kindreds." [1]

Similarly, Eduard Meyer in his definition of the state stresses the notion of absolute dominance: all individuals, all lesser social groups are subordinated, if necessary by force; there is unity of will, maintenance of legal order, military and political organization, and above all the consciousness of the permanence of the unit independently of the will of its individual members or its lesser groups (*das*

[1] Paul Vinogradoff, *Outlines of Historical Jurisprudence* (1920), I: 93.

Bewusstsein der Ewigkeit des Verbandes, dessen Bestand von dem Willen der zu ihm gehörigen Unterabteilungen und Individuen unabhängig ist, wohl aber diese unter seinen Willen zwingt).[2]

There is nevertheless a fundamental difference between the two authors. While Vinogradoff emphatically denies the existence of sovereignty in ancient civilizations, let alone, on lower levels of culture, Meyer vehemently affirms its presence even among nomadic and hunting tribes. As a matter of fact, Meyer considers the state, as he defines it, the equivalent of the herd among lower species; for him, consequently, it is the primeval social unit, older than the human species, whose evolution was only made possible by its means.

Now, as indicated in the Introduction, I wholly assent to Meyer's view that some sort of state is a universal feature of human culture. But I also insist that this proposition can be defended only on a quite different basis of definition. Meyer's theory results clearly from his glorification of one particular type of state, which to thinkers of other schools of political science is not only unacceptable but revolting. Even so moderate a writer as Professor L. Duguit postulates as an ideal consistent with the soundest regulation of political affairs in civilized countries a *decentralized* society in which a mod-

[2] Meyer, *Geschichte des Altertums* (1907), *Erste Hälfte*, I: 10–12.

icum of state surveillance shall be coupled with an organization into fairly independent occupational groups.[3]

But, whatever may be the psychological basis of Meyer's theory, an analysis of the empirical data lends no support to his conception of an omnipresent "unity of will" or "consciousness of the permanence of the social unit." As he himself admits, medieval history shows that the unified state is a painfully slow development from very modest germs. Where did sovereignty lodge in Scandinavia when a king, on his accession to the throne, was obliged to travel from province to province to gain the acknowledgment of local assemblies? In Iceland the Althing was an assembly of freemen who passed laws but had no power to enforce them; while the Lawman elected by the legislature merely recited the code and served as chairman, but neither pronounced judgment nor inflicted punishment, exercising his functions solely during the meetings themselves.[4] As for the continent, Vinogradoff has pointed out by what laborious steps the state acquired its coercive potency through the stages of compulsory arbitration, self-help, and outlawry. Even in Charlemagne's day it was only in specific cases that the central authority executed one of its own decrees.

[3] *Le Droit Social* (1911).
[4] Mary Wilhelmine Williams, *Social Scandinavia in the Viking Age* (1920), 271 *seq.*, 290.

A still more impressive though less generally known illustration is provided by the history of the Chinese Empire, for this immense country succeeded in maintaining its ancient cultural tradition with a very minimum of "sovereignty." It is true that in theory the Emperor was the patriarchal ruler over all, the vicegerent of Heaven, the fountainhead of power, rank and authority, that he was surrounded by a pretentious court, claimed implicit obedience from his subjects, and was in no wise obliged to take cognizance of their rights. To quote S. W. Williams for the period of forty odd years ago, "Liberty is unknown among the people, there is not even a word for it in the language."

However, to scan Williams' own account more closely is to discover that he has committed the common error of confounding legal theory with fact.

In reality the putative autocrat was bound to rule according to the codified law of the land, which was newly edited every five years; the nobility surrounding him derived neither power, land, office, nor influence from their honors; his own sons and kindred were excluded from civil office in the provinces; while his official acts were recorded by a Board of Censors who were not afraid of openly reproving him for any deviation from the traditional path of duty. Thus, Sung denounced Kiaking for his attachment to actors and drink, "which

degraded him in the eyes of his people and in-
capacitated him for performing his duties"; while
another censor rebuked an emperor of the Tang
dynasty for wanting to inspect the Board's records.[5]

In fact, if we consider the actual working of the
governmental scheme as described by Williams,
Giles, and others, Williams's summary appears ludicrously wide of the mark. While in theory the viceroys and governors of the eighteen provinces were
responsible to the central government at Peking, the
Emperor being accountable only to Heaven, these
provincial viceroys were normally to all intents and
purposes independent rulers. As for the people at
large, they looked for official guidance primarily
to the district magistrates, men who had taken the
third degree of scholarship and who served as coro-
ners, taxcollectors, registrars of land conveyances,
suppliants for rain, and as preliminary examiners.
National sentiment was nonexistent. To quote M.
Courant, "*Pour le Chinois, la patrie n'est pas l'Empire,
mais la province, plutôt encore le district d'où il est
originaire.*"

As for liberty, the Chinese were far from being
the downtrodden slaves portrayed by Williams. We
read how the populace killed a cruel prefect, sooth-
ing their civic consciences by the facile rationalization that he had acted contrary to the Emperor's

[5] S. W. Williams, *The Middle Kingdom* (1883), 2 vols., I: 380–431.

benevolent intentions.   Again, when in 1838 the
governor of Canton tried to search all shops in a
street for opium, the shopmen in a body went to
the entrance of the thoroughfare and told the police
they would under no condition permit the search; and
the govenor deemed it wise to recede from his position. Or, take the typical case of the taxgatherer
imprisoned by a magistrate for being in arrears.
His wife rushed to the office, demanding his re-
lease, and being asthmatic died on the spot. The people at once wrecked the office and beat the official,
who had to flee in disguise. Still more instructive is the history of a mandarin who kicked and
killed a weakly lad. His mother sat down before
the house, surrounded by her sympathizers. A deputy magistrate investigated the case and announced
that the youth had died by accident. The crowd
forthwith smashed his sedan, manhandled the official, thrust him into the rice fields, and remained
to see what would happen in the interests of justice.
The viceroy was obliged to take cognizance of the
affair, dispatching a new deputy. This official held
an inquest at 10 A. M. and at 11 the offending mandarin's head was cut off. Then the crowd dispersed.
    Most illuminating of all, however, is the tale of
how new taxes were imposed under the imperial
rule during the last century. According to Giles,
the local magistrate would send for the village head-

men or leading merchants and discuss the proposed
measure over tea and the smoking of tobacco. After much debating pro and con, a compromise was
usually reached. Failing this, the magistrate might
attempt force. Thus, in 1880 one of these officials
issued a proclamation that a tax of 200 cash would
be imposed on every pig killed by the butchers.
These resolved not to kill pigs until the ordinance
was abrogated; a party of them went about town
and seized all the pork exposed for sale. Then the
five hundred members of the trade shut themselves
up in their guild house, where the magistrate, ac-
companied by from two to three hundred runners,
vainly attempted to force an entrance. Public
opinion at once veered against the official for having taken this step. Three days later *all* the shops
of the town were closed, the people being afraid
of hostilities and robbery. Two days later the
butchers were still holding their fort, refusing to do
business, while the prefect exhorted the merchants
to open their shops. On the following day he issued
a proclamation, apologizing to the people and, more
particularly to the butchers. "So the officials,"
Giles concludes his diary record, "have all miser-
ably failed in squeezing a *cash* out of the 'sovereign people' of Ssu'ch'wan." [6]

[6] Williams, *op. cit.*, I: 488, 506. H. A. Giles, *China and the Chinese*
(1902), 75–106. Maurice Courant, *En Chine* (1901), 68.

In all this there is no trace of subordination under a supreme will transcending that of the individual members of the state, no sense of that eternity of the national tie which figures in Meyer's conception. We shall hardly assume that this sentiment appears in hypertrophied form among the ruder, unsettled tribes of the globe.

At the same time the principle of continuity suggests that the *germs* of sovereignty may and must be present even on so lowly a level as the Andamanese, where indeed the attitude of each group in excluding trespassers may be taken as foreshadowing territorial sovereignty. We shall see that this principle does assert itself more or less sporadically and inconsistently in primitive society and may sometimes even approach the modern ideal. But sovereignty in the metaphysical sense assigned by Meyer must be relegated to its proper place in anthropological perspective, as a limiting concept realized only under definite conditions and forming a special and minor part of the general problem.

It is clear from Meyer's statements that he was partly led astray by reaction against the dogma that in early societies the place of the state was wholly taken by groups of blood kindred. We shall see presently that this is by no means the sole alternative.

IV

THE TERRITORIAL TIE

In 1861 Sir Henry Sumner Maine, the father of comparative jurisprudence, sharply separated two principles of uniting individuals for governmental purposes,—the blood tie and the territorial tie. He further combined this conceptual distinction with an *historical* theory, to wit, that in less advanced or earlier societies "kinship in blood is the sole possible ground of community in political functions." No revolution, he argued, could be "so startling and so complete as the change which is accomplished when some other principle—such as that, for instance, of *local contiguity*—establishes itself for the first time as the basis of common political action." And, again, he writes: " . . . the idea that a number of persons should exercise political rights in common simply because they happened to live within the same topographical limits was utterly strange and monstrous to primitive antiquity." Where members of alien lineage were taken into the fold it was at least on the basis of a legal fiction that they were "descended from the same stock as the people on whom they were engrafted." [1]

[1] *Ancient Law*, Chapter V, 124-126.

51

When Lewis H. Morgan developed his own scheme of "Ancient Society" (1877), he not only adopted Maine's basic distinction but also gave greater definiteness to the views of his predecessor, especially in point of chronology. All forms of government, he argued, belonged to one of two categories,—they were either founded on persons and personal relations or on territory and property. Ranged on one side were such units as the gens (clan, sib) and phratry; on the other, the series comprising the ward, township, county, province, and national domain. Political, that is, territorial organization was declared to have been unknown prior to classical antiquity. It was in 594 B. C. that Solon took the initial step of breaking up the patrilineal gentes (clans, sibs) of the Athenians by a property classification, and in 507 B. C. Cleisthenes completed the advance by substituting for the traditional gentile organization purely local lines of division, by cutting up the old noble lineages and assigning the fragments to different local groups. Henceforth every citizen was registered, taxed, and given a vote as a member not of a clan but of a township, that is, of a territorial unit.

This classical distinction between "social" or "tribal", and "political" or "territorial", organization is significant and unexceptionable. That is to say, there *is* a fundamental difference between the two principles discriminated, and of both the history of human society provides abundant examples. It is not the logical but the historical aspect of the theory that evokes doubt. Why should the peoples of the world, after contentedly living for millennia under a government based on the blood tie, engage in that startling revolution described by Maine, of substituting the totally novel alignment of persons by locality? Neither author provides an adequate solution. Must we here break with the notion of continuous evolution? That certainly grates on the sensibilities of latter-day historical-mindedness. In the presence of overwhelming positive evidence we should be willing to cast Continuity on the rubbish heap of exploded fictions, but without such rigorous demonstration we shall do well to cling to it and seek an alternative interpretation. Nor is it difficult to outline the avenue of approach. If 507 or 594 B. C. does *not* mark an abrupt departure from past tradition, then older and simpler communities must have displayed the local bond along with the consanguineal tie. The two principles, in other words, however antithetical, are not of necessity mutually exclusive. It is then possible to satisfy the postulate of Continuity. We are no longer face to face with the miracle of a spontaneous generation but with the scientific problem of how an originally weak but perceptible territorial sentiment, at first subordinate to the blood tie, was intensified to the point of assuming the dominant rôle.

Whether this interpretation is warranted, is of course a question to be determined by empirical facts.

In fairness we must, first of all, concede that these yield considerable justification for the position maintained by Maine and Morgan. Again and again, in going over the descriptive literature of social anthropology, the reader must be struck by the prominence of personal relationship in governmental affairs, such as the administration of justice. What, for instance, is the significance of the blood feud, which outside of Africa is such a common mode of adjusting misunderstandings? From the present angle it is simply a negation of the state: it implies the doctrine that persons living in the same village or country are not by such juxtaposition jointly subordinate to some transcendent local authority but have claims upon and obligations to their kin only, each lineage standing towards any other in the same relationship as, say, the United States to France or England,—perhaps actually at amity, yet at any time potentially shifting into a state of avowed hostility.

The condition thus abstractly defined is best illustrated by a series of examples taken from different parts of the primitive world.

Let us begin with the Yurok of northwestern California. We have already commented on the smallness of their political units; at present we are concerned with their composition. Examining one of the typical hamlets, such as Weitspus on the Klamath River, we find an aggregation of less than 200 souls, the male population comprising mainly or exclusively blood kindred. The women generally come from other settlements; apart from this tendency to "local exogamy", the village is a self-contained, independent center of population lacking a sense of attachment to any equivalent units, or of subordination to a major whole, and to that extent comparable with an Andamanese camp. Of adjacent settlements in a group, one "was sometimes involved in a feud while another directly across the river looked on." Indeed, even within the hamlet itself a communal sense is lacking: the individual Weitspus recognizes no duty to his fellow-townsfolk, no executive or judicial authority; his obligations are to his kin and his kin only, so that "all so-called wars were only feuds that happened to involve large groups of kinsmen, several such groups, or unrelated fellow townsmen of the original participants." Notwithstanding the complete absence of administrative and legal officials, the Yurok have a definite code of customary laws; yet all "rights, claims, possessions, and privileges are individual and personal, and all wrongs are

against individuals. There is no offense against the
community, no duty owing it, no right or power of
any sort inhering in it." And, as a corollary to this
proposition, punishment of a public character is likewise wanting. "Each side to an issue presses and
resists vigorously, exacts all it can, yields when it
has to, continues the controversy when continuance
promises to be profitable or settlement is clearly suici-
dal, and usually ends in compromising more or less." [2]

This description is, *mutatis mutandis*, wholly appli-
cable to the Angami Naga, who occupy the hills between Assam and Burma. Though living in a village,
the Angami looks upon the sib (clan) as the real unit
of organization. "So distinct is the clan from the
village that it forms almost a village in itself, often
fortified within the village inside in its own bound-
aries and not infrequently at variance almost amount-
ing to war with other clans in the same village.
Under normal circumstances there are sporadic riots
due to the internal dissensions between the kin
groups since in most disputes between two men of
different clans the clansmen on each side appear as
partisans and foment the discord." Even in times
of war clan jealousies prove a disruptive force.[3]

Perhaps a still more striking illustration is supplied by the Ifugao of northern Luzon, precisely

[2] Kroeber, *Handbook of the Indians of California* (1925), 3, 8–15, 20, 49.
[3] J. H. Hutton, *The Angami Nagas* (1921), 109.

because these Philippine Islanders exemplify the paradox of an exceedingly complicated body of customary law coupled with a condition of virtual anarchy. Our principal source, Dr. R. F. Barton,[4] is quite clear-cut on the subject. He represents the natives as acting with complete disregard of any considerations outside of relationship. An individual owes support to his kindred against all other kin groups, and in proportion to the proximity of his relationship, while he is free from any obligations to the remainder of the local group. This group has no authorized official to arrange disputes between distinct bodies of kindred; there is merely a go-between with purely advisory functions. According to the author's explicit interpretation the political life of the Ifugao rests on consanguinity, and on consanguinity only.

The three examples cited in some measure justify the views of Maine and Morgan. Here are three peoples remote from one another and described by as many independent witnesses, whose testimony agrees as to the point at issue. Nevertheless, a closer scrutiny of the evidence reveals in each and every one of these instances that while the blood tie is the conspicuous one the local bond is by no means wholly in abeyance.

[4] *Ifugao Law*, in *Univ. of Cal. Pub. in Amer. Arch. and Ethnol.* (1919), XV: 1–127.

Let us begin by examining the Ifugao, on whom the descriptive material is most abundant. We find, first of all, that throughout Ifugao territory there is substantial agreement as to customary law. The principles on which a go-between intermediating between warring families renders his decision enjoy general acceptance, even though they may be warped in particular applications. In cases of adultery a fine is imposed on the offender, the amount varying with the relative status in society of the aggrieved and the guilty party. That *some* penalty should be inflicted, is acknowledged even by the offender and his relatives; they are merely leagued together to shield him from bodily harm and beat down exorbitant demands for indemnity. Even if the adulterer is a prominent man supported by a host of henchmen he does not seek wholly to evade punishment but only to reduce it to a minimum. In short, there *is* definite recognition of some obligations to *un*related members of the same community. This rudimentary sense of duty toward the local group stands forth most clearly in the treatment of thieves. If Barton's picture of Ifugao society were to be taken literally, we should expect the same punishment to be meted out to *any* person outside the aggrieved party's kindred. But this inference does not tally with the facts reported. Theft committed by a fellow villager is mulcted by a traditional fine; a marauding outsider, however, is almost certain to be slain forthwith. Similarly, the principle of collective responsibility is extended beyond the circle of consanguinity so as to embrace the neighborhood group. If a creditor remains unsatisfied, he may on occasion appropriate buffalo belonging not only to his tardy debtor or his kin but those of any person inhabiting the same village.

Finally, there is a tacit understanding among different kin groups that internecine strife should be discountenanced lest the *territorial* unit be unduly weakened as compared with corresponding units; and the individual Ifugao is expected to comport himself in such fashion as not to entangle his neighbors in hostilities with other *local* groups. In short, the apparently exclusive potency of blood relationship is seen to be appreciably limited by the recognition of local contiguity as a basis for political action and sentiment.

What is true of the Ifugao, holds likewise for the equally "anarchic" Yurok. Professor Kroeber successfully disproves the existence of any *national* sentiment among them in his account of their so-called wars, which would fail to unite more than one tenth of the whole "tribe" against, say, the Hupa. But the same narratives also show that local affiliations of lesser scope were operative:

"under threat of attack from a remote and consolidated alien foe, village might adhere to village
in joint war, just as, in lesser feuds, town mates,
impelled by bonds of association or imperiled by
their common residence, would sometimes unite
with the group of individuals with whom the feud
originated." Our author adds that "these are
occasions such as draw neighbors together the
world over, be they individuals, districts, or nations." But that is precisely my contention, to
wit, that even in extreme cases of separatism the
neighborhood tie becomes a significant element in
governmental activity, not perhaps in itself adequate for the institution of what we call "political" organization but providing the germ from
which such an organization may develop.

This factor is strengthened by two features. For
one thing, the men of a settlement are united by
the institution of the sudatory, where they both
sweat and sleep together throughout the winter
and often in the summer, "passing the evenings in
talk and smoking." The type of social unit thus
created will be discussed more fully in the following chapter. Secondly, the local tie clearly appears in ritualistic activity. Not only is each ceremony riveted to a particular spot but, what is far
more important in the present context, the association with localities serves to knit people together.

Every main performance is conducted by competing parties representing as many villages. "These match and outdo one another, as the rich man of each village gradually hands over more and more of his own and his followers' and friends' valuables to the dancers to display." Moreover, it may be said that the very fact of such amicable rivalry in some manner counteracts the excessive particularism described above. It might have paved the way, though apparently among the Yurok it never did, for a more extensive union of local bodies.[5]

Angami conditions are amazingly like those reported for the Yurok and the Ifugao. On the one hand, the same centrifugal tendency is expressed in exaggeratedly tangible form, so that one clan in the village may be separated from the rest by a wall twelve feet in thickness. Murder leads to a vendetta waged by the clans concerned rather than to the expulsion of the criminal by a judicial authority, and in cases of misunderstanding between persons of different villages the blood feud might be restricted to the kindred of the two parties "and it would be quite possible for all the other clans in both villages to be friendly, while the clans of the respective parties to the vendetta were on head-taking terms." Nevertheless, when a serious breach of the social code occurs "the clans in almost any

[5] Kroeber, *op. cit.*, 15, 50, 55, 81.

village would be found agreed"; military operations are certainly carried on by villagers as such;
and many important magico-religious observances
are communal in character.[6]

The Yurok, Ifugao and Angami are *a fortiori*
instances: they represent the maximum conceivable
lack of governmental coördination of the kin
groups occupying the same habitat. If even here
the traditional theory of the exclusiveness of the
blood tie breaks down, the presence of the local
bond will have to be admitted for less extreme cases.
However, it is possible to go further and to turn
the tables on Maine and Morgan. Not only do
local ties coexist with those of blood kinship, but
it may be contended that the bond of relationship when defined in sociological rather than biological terms is itself in no small part a *derivative*
of local contiguity. This view is so contrary to
accepted notions that some evidence must be ad-
duced in its defense.

Let us once more turn to the Angami Naga.
Like many of the ruder peoples, they are divided
into moieties, each child being reckoned from birth
either a Pezoma or a Pepfüma according to his
father's half of the tribe. This dual organization
is traced to two legendary brothers, whose respective descendants the members of the two subdivisions

---

[6] Hutton, *op. cit.*, 45, 109, 150 *seq.*, 193.

are believed to be. But unlike such lineages elsewhere, the Angami moieties are not exogamous
at the present time: often the population of a village
is composed wholly of persons of one moiety and
no objection is voiced against the marriage of
fellow members. It is credibly stated by Mr. Hutton's informants that the customary taboo once
held sway, but in course of time there seems to
have been a constant shift of the marriage regulating function to lesser and lesser fragments of
the moiety. Thus, the village of Kohima is in-
habited exclusively by Pepfüma people, who freely
intermarry so far as they belong to distinct sibs.
Of these, at one time within native tradition, there
were only two, *viz.*, the Cherama and the Pferonoma.
These, accordingly, were at that time to all intents
and purposes exogamous moieties on the familiar
pattern, as Pezoma and Pepfüma are reputed to
have once been. But while Cherama persisted
unsegmented, its mate was broken up into six
sections, making (with Cherama) seven sibs in all
at the present time. The exogamous unit of Kohima
has thus been repeatedly redefined: at first it
was presumably the archaic Pepfüma moiety, whose
members were forced to seek spouses outside their
own village; subsequently fellow-Pepfüma might
marry, provided the union was that of a Cherama
with a Pferonoma; and finally, a Pferonoma of sib

a might marry either a Cherama or a Pferonoma of sibs *b, c, d, e, f.*

Nevertheless, so far there is no deviation from the widespread principle that marriage is regulated by *some* sort of kinship body, though the incest group, to use a convenient term, has materially shrunk in course of time. When, however, we scrutinize the data of Mr. Hutton's genealogical tables and his accompanying text, a new fact of the utmost importance emerges. *Permissible inter-marriage is a function of locality no less than of consanguinity.* That is to say, the more inclusive kinship taboo is relaxed only in so far as the individuals concerned are not coresidents in the same community. To quote some striking sentences from our author's report:

"The marriage in the present generation is Pezoma-Pezoma, but *between different villages.*"

"Here there is a Pezoma-Pezoma marriage in the last generation and a Pepfüma-Pepfüma marriage in the generation before, but in the latter case *between persons of different villages.*"

The Cherhechima division "may not intermarry within itself *in the same village.*" [7]

The kin group, in short, is not a marriage regulating group simply because it is a kin group but partly, at least, because it is a local group.

[7] Hutton, *op. cit.*, 110 *seq.*, 125–132, 418 *seq.* The italics are mine.

This interpretation, however, may be challenged on the ground that the territorial factor came to be stressed at a relatively late stage, while in the earlier periods the patrilineal kin group was the sole principle regulating sex relations. It might also be contended that even today the intrusion of the local factor is incidental or derivative: exogamy is local only because within the settlement there is certainty as to blood kinship while people living elsewhere are either not known to be related or known to be only remotely related. This argument is plausible enough, and in order to meet it we must proceed to a critique of the kinship concept itself.

While kinship is universally recognized between a child and both his parents, this resulting "bilateral" kin group corresponding to our own family is frequently supplemented among the simpler peoples of the globe by the familiar "unilateral" kin. That is to say, the child is linked either with the father *or* the mother, the Angami illustrating the patrilineal, the Hopi of Arizona the matrilineal variety of unilateral reckoning. Since the bilateral family is omnipresent, this may seem to involve a contradiction, which, nevertheless, is more apparent than real. The bilateral family may, for instance, center in certain economic duties and sentimental attachments, while political functions—

say, the blood feud—are connected solely with
the patrilineal group.

Now, my contention is that both the bilateral
(family) and the unilateral (clan, sib, moiety)
unit are rooted in a local as well as a consanguine
factor. Let us begin by considering the unilateral
kin group, which in some quarters is still regarded as
a distinguishing badge of primitive society generally.

Among the unilaterally organized tribes there
are some in which the kin and the territorial group
coincide. This is true of large sections of California.
Mr. Gifford has recently shown that the Miwok,
who live near the center of the state, were formerly
split up into minute paternal lineages, each politically autonomous, each bearing a local name and
owning a definite tract of land. Closely conforming
to this model, the South Californian Diegueño
were organized into patrilineal groups controlling
areas so definitely circumscribed that it has been
possible to plot their respective holdings. Similarly, in West Australia the local group embraces
a body of blood relatives related through their
fathers, and it is this small group, simultaneously
consanguine and territorial, that acts as a miniature state, for example, by waging war.[8]

[8] E. W. Gifford, *Miwok Lineages and the Political Unit in Aboriginal
California*, in *American Anthropologist* (1926), 389–401. L. Spier,
Southern Diegueño Customs, in *Univ. Cal. Publs. Amer. Arch. and Ethnol.*
(1923), XX: 296–308. R. H. Lowie, *Primitive Society* (1920), 393.

Now, what makes a group of this type cohere? It is easy to say that the sense of blood relationship is primary, but very difficult to prove; for what we observe is not such priority but the inextricable union of the consanguine and the local bond. Each unit in West Australia feels itself indissolubly linked with a definite locality by mystical ties. Why? Because of the reverence felt for the paternal ancestry settled there? But why *should* the paternal ancestry be singled out for reverential treatment? Is it not possible to invert the cheap and obvious explanation? It may be that the aborigines do not view a locality reverently because it is connected with their paternal ancestors but that they esteem their ancestors in so far as they are linked with a certain locality.

This leads us directly to the core of the clan problem. Why, we ask, do people ever feel a more special affiliation with one side of the family than with the other? It cannot be the kinship factor that accounts for the differential relationship, for that factor would operate equally for the paternal and the maternal kindred. The clue to the solution was long ago supplied by E. B. Tylor.[9] Let us assume the rule of marriage that obtains among the Hopi of Arizona,—matrilocal residence. By this the bridegroom takes up his abode with his

---

[9] *The Matriarchal Family System*, in *Nineteenth Century* (1896), 91–96.

wife's parents, that is to say, since there is female house ownership, with his mother-in-law, to whom her other daughters likewise bring their several husbands. This explains forthwith why kinsfolk biologically on a par are discriminated sociologically. Between the mother's brother, who sees his sisters' children grow up under his own mother's roof, and his nephews and nieces there naturally develops a sentiment of attachment that cannot possibly obtain between them and the father's brother. Similarly, the mother's sister becomes a closer relation than the paternal aunt, who cannot possibly be a coresident. It is equally clear why there is a discrimination between different types of cousin. A Hopi grows up with the children of his mother's sister, while the children of his *father's* sister are reared in another house. In corresponding fashion the scales are weighted in favor of the *paternal* kin wherever patrilocal residence takes the place of matrilocalism. In short, spatial segregation accounts to a large extent for the alignment of relatives found in a tribe organized into clans.

It is true that residence after marriage is not always rigidly or permanently fixed, and in such cases supplementary factors must be invoked. For instance, a paternal lineage may be linked, as in northeastern North America, by common utilization of a hunting territory. Again, as in sections of Australia, a maternal kin group may cohere through exploitation of the same seed gathering tract; or, as among the Hidatsa, by the joint cultivation of a plot by a mother, her daughters, and her daughters' daughters. But in each of these instances, the ultimate determinant of cohesion is evidently not mere kinship but kinship enforced by propinquity.

So far I have considered the blood bond only with reference to the unilateral kinship group which looms so large in the discussions of ancient law. At present, however, it is recognized by all ethnologists open to argument that the unilateral principle is not a primeval one but was superimposed at a relatively late period upon the bilateral principle, which invariably accompanies it. The evidence from nearly all the unequivocally simplest tribes of the globe, such as the Shoshoneans of Utah and Nevada, the Yahgan of Tierra del Fuego, the Andamanese of the Bay of Bengal, and the Chukchi of northeastern Siberia seems to dispose of the hoary dogma that the clan is a truly archaic institution. [10] If, then, the basic importance of the local element is to be established, it must be demonstrated not only in association with the unilateral clan but with the bilateral family.

[10] R. H. Lowie, *Primitive Society* (1920), 150 *seq.* W. Schmidt, *Völker und Kulturen* (1924), 79 *seq.*

The very attempt to do this may seem fantastic; for how can anything claim equal rank with those fundamental blood ties upon which our very existence depends? Here, however, we must stress a point of the utmost importance, which has been recently expressed by Dr. Malinowski. Biological and sociological kinship are two distinct concepts. The one is based on instinctive response in accordance with biological utility; the other, however dependent for its origin on the former, is never wholly derived from it and may diverge from it very appreciably. As Malinowski insists, the maternal *instinct* ceases with the discharge of its biological functions; it becomes a *sociologically* creative force only when it has ripened into a specifically human "sentiment" in Shand's sense of the term. But what is it, I should ask, that fosters the sentiment unless it is the constant association during childhood,—prolonged in primitive communities by the generally extended period of lactation? Eliminate the element of contiguity, and the family as a *social* unit tends to disappear. Bogoras's graphic picture of Chukchi life introduces us to lone boys wandering away from home never to return. In what sense do they remain members of their families? Evidently only in a biological sense; sociologically the tie snaps when it fails to be reënforced by spatial proximity.

As for the bond between father and child, we

have that whole range of usages which obscure biological paternity while in no way affecting the social or legal kinship. The case of the Bánaro, who
live along the Potter's River in New Guinea, has
been thoroughly elucidated by Dr. Thurnwald and
may serve for purposes of illustration.[11] A Bánaro
bride is not initiated into the mysteries of sex life by
her husband, but by a friend of her husband's father
and, subsequently, by her father-in-law. These activities take place in the so-called spirit hall of the
village, and the men themselves are said to imper-
sonate a spirit. As for the groom, he is not permitted
access to his wife until after the birth of a child,
which is designated as a "spirit's child" (*Geisterkind*)
but is adopted by his mother's husband. Owing to
the ceremonial laxity of sex relations during great
tribal festivals, the husband cannot even be certain
of his paternity in the case of subsequent issue. But,
as our authority again and again assures us, this
is a matter of complete indifference to the natives:
"*Ob der Gatte der wirkliche Vater der Kinder ist,
kommt bei diesem System nicht in Betracht.*" The concept of fatherhood is linked with that not of pro-
creator but of educator, provider and protector. It is
the husband's cohabitation with the mother—in the
etymological no less than in the customary sense of

[11] Thurnwald, *Die Gemeinde der Bânaro* (Stuttgart, 1921), pp. 21
seq., 37 *f.*, 99 *seq.*

the term—that stamps him sociologically as a parent and makes the children members of *his* clan. Kinship is not kinship in its own right, but as a derivative of a local factor. As Dr. Malinowski has put it, there seems to be a "tendency in the human species, on the part of the male to feel attached to the children born by a woman with whom he has mated, has been living permanently and has kept watch over during her pregnancy."[12]

Dr. Thurnwald's Papuan case is but a special sample of the wider category of adoption,—that legal fiction by which children who need not even be related may become, for all social purposes, as their adoptive parents' real offspring. Whatever may be the motive in different areas, which presumably varies considerably, the psychological concomitant is usually a sentimental relationship that approximates, if it does not attain, the natural emotions. The data from other areas seem to me to corroborate my personal impression among the Crow Indians, that there is a generic love of children—no matter whose—which merely requires to be particularized in a definite instance by constant association in order to develop into a full-fledged parental sentiment.

To sum up our argument. The traditional distinction established by Maine and Morgan retains

[12] B. Malinowski, *Crime and Custom in Savage Society* (1926), 107.

its validity in so far as conceptually a union of neighbors is different from a union of kinsmen. It must even be conceded that the blood tie is frequently the overshadowing element in the governmental activities of primitive peoples. Yet, though it often dwarfs the territorial factor, it never succeeds in eliminating it. Nay, if we inquire into the bond of consanguinity itself, we find lurking in the background a spatial determinant of the sentiments underlying it. Abstractly separated by a chasm, the two types of union are in reality intertwined. The basic problem of the state is thus not that of explaining the somersault by which ancient peoples achieved the step from a government by personal relations to one by territorial contiguity only. The question is rather to show what processes strengthened the local tie which must be recognized as not less ancient than the rival principle.

V

ASSOCIATIONS

At this point it is necessary to evaluate the state-building potency of a type of social activity wholly ignored by the older theorists, to wit, the units called "associations." In Professor Maciver's definition an association "is an organization of social beings . . . . . for the pursuit of some common interest or interests."[1] This author emphasizes the fact that such a group is not a random aggregation like a crowd of spectators at a fire, but a group consolidated by a common end. For anthropological purposes we may conveniently restrict the term to such units in so far as they are not primarily based on either the blood tie or the territorial tie since generally intelligible terms are in vogue for both the several kinship and the local groups. Incidentally, of course, or secondarily, it is quite possible for the consanguineal and the local factor to be connected with the associational. For example, among the Yoruba of West Africa a man "always joins the particular society of which his ancestors were members, and the population of most towns

[1] *Community* (1924), 23 *seq.*

74

belong generally either to one or the other."[2]
But the associations in question are not composed
either of a single lineage or of a single local group:
they comprise various families and various towns.
What unites all the people in, say, the Oro association is the common worship of a distinctive deity
and the joint performance of certain funeral ceremonies, irrespective of either kinship or residence.
The older theorists on primitive social organization were intent on tracing the evolution of the
blood tie, hence one may read a book like Morgan's
Ancient Society from cover to cover without di-
vining that Melanesia, West Africa, and large
areas in America were honeycombed with social
units in no way, or at best indirectly, connected
with the clan ("gentile," sib) bond. This is all the
more remarkable because the writings of naïve observers long antedating the theorists in question frequently record the occurrence of associations. As
early as 1670 O. Dapper's *Umbständliche und Eigent-
liche Beschreibung von Africa* records the narratives
of seafaring men concerning the secret men's and
women's societies of the West African Vai.[3] Hennepin (1680) describes a police organization among
the Dakota Indians, while Lewis and Clark's *Jour-*

[2] P. Amaury Talbot, *The Peoples of Southern Nigeria* (1926), III: 758.
[3] Diedrich Westermann, *Die Kpelle, ein Negerstamm in Liberia* (1921),
265.

nals (1804) report Dakota and Crow societies. To mention only one other instance from still another region, the Areoi of the Tahitians is clearly described in the South Sea Island literature of the eighteenth century. But it was not before 1902 that Heinrich Schurtz remedied the serious deficiency of theoretical sociology due to the neglect of such phenomena by publishing his comprehensive work on *Altersklassen und Männerbünde*. Six years later Professor Hutton Webster issued a similarly documented book on *Primitive Secret Societies;* and quite recently Father Schmidt has elaborated some individual interpretations of the subject in his *Völker und Kulturen* (1924).

A full treatment of associations, summarizing the descriptive material published up to date and doing full justice to the historical and psychological questions involved, would require several volumes. Here we are interested only in investigating the connection of associations with the state. That is to say, our inquiry is directed towards determining in how far associations, which ostensibly and primarily serve specific purposes of their own, incidentally tend to organize society on territorial lines. But in order to gain an insight into this problem, it will be necessary to make a rapid ethnographic survey of associations with special reference to the basis of membership.

First of all, then, every society is sociologically divided along sex lines. Apart from those activities which must biologically devolve on the men or the women there is a traditional division of labor that, however deeprooted and tenaciously clung to, might just as well be reversed. Among the Palikur of Brazilian Guiana the women make pottery, weave, and crochet, while the men make baskets; and though either sex may catch fish with a line and hook, to stupefy them with poison is a masculine prerogative. In Uganda, British East Africa, all the horticultural work is done by women except that men always plant the trees yielding bark cloth. In Africa the manufacture of bark cloth devolves on the men, in Polynesia on the women. Sometimes even neighboring tribes differ in their conception of masculine and feminine tasks: it is the men among the Hopi of Arizona but the Navaho women that weave cloth. On the other hand, some industries—such as hand-made pottery—are rather uniformly in the hands of women. In short, the biological duality of every community is correlated with an informal grouping in occupational sex moieties.

This dichotomy, however, may become formally organized by a far-reaching segregation of the sexes in social and religious activities. Either, as in Australia, Melanesia, and New Guinea, women may be simply barred from a tribal society including all adult males; or, as in Africa, each sex has its distinctive organization, from which the other is strictly excluded. Among the Banks Islanders the men have their own fraternity house, which serves as their regular dormitory, refectory, workshop and lounging place. The women have dwellings of their own, where they are visited by their husbands while the clubhouse, the center of ceremonial and political life, remains taboo to them. Elsewhere the separation is less thoroughgoing but equally strict so far as it goes: in many South American tribes, for example, men and women never eat together, while in northwestern California the men sleep apart from their wives during the winter season.

In many tribes this sex dichotomy is replaced or supplemented by segregation on the basis of age or status. The entire population may be split up into a series of groups differing by age, matrimonial status, etc., and these differences may be tangibly expressed by distinctive dress, decoration, food taboos, or residence. In the Andaman Islands and Australia there is a bachelors' camp separate from the huts of the married couples. Among the Masai there are three status grades, those of the uninitiated, of the initiated but as yet unmarried, and of the married. In addition, all those initiated

within the same four year period form a permanent
union.

It is of course a characteristic of the age grade
proper that "every member of the community passes
automatically through the consecutive groups." [4]
But sometimes extraneous elements intrude to
alter the basic character of these associations.
Among the Ibo of the lower Niger, there are eight
classes, the lowest and the highest being still clearly
age groups. But in the intermediate ones the
age factor has been blurred, so that a wealthy man
may *buy* promotion for his son into the second
highest class.[5] In Benin, the capital of the empire
of Bini, there were four societies in which the members were always succeeded by their eldest sons;
but comparison with the conditions prevailing
in the rest of the country strongly suggests that
these are merely transformed age classes.[6] The
tribal men's and women's societies of various African
peoples seem to be the direct outgrowth of the
initiation rites at puberty, *i. e.*, of the status units
formed by admission to the position of an adult.[7]

But the basis of membership may be utterly
different from any of the foregoing. In parts of
Southern Nigeria "no man could become a member

[4] Talbot, *op. cit.*, III: 544.
[5] *Ibid.*, 549.
[6] Talbot, *op. cit.*, III: 545.
[7] Westermann, *op. cit.*, 234–253.

of the senior club unless he could produce the head of an enemy slain by him"; and the chief association among the Semi-Bantu of the area was originally a society of diviners, though later it became open on payment of an admission fee.[8]   The Omaha of Nebraska and the Dakota Indians had associations of men united by a similar vision, say, of the buffalo or the elk.   Finally, there are societies that can be entered by free choice, as in the case of certain military organizations of the Plains Indians.

Now, it hardly requires close scrutiny to see that these various types of association have a very unequal bearing on governmental development. It remains, however, to define with some precision, which associations are, and which are not, of a potentially political character; and this problem can perhaps be solved by an intensive consideration of two areas for which descriptive material is fairly abundant.

KPELLE ASSOCIATIONS [9]

The Kpelle are a horticultural Sudanese people linguistically related to the Mande (Mandingo) and occupying mainly the left bank of Paul River in Liberia.   Secret societies dominate their life, for membership in them is prerequisite to marriage, to

---

[8] Talbot, op. cit., 788, 790.
[9] Westermann, Die Kpelle (1921), 4, 12, 228-290.

office, to participation in religious activity and even to honorable burial. Residence becomes almost intolerable for the uninitiated, so that even aliens seek admission in order to enhance their status.

Among the Kpelle proper there are six associations of varying importance and character. Foremost stands the Poro, into which all boys enter at the age of from seven to fifteen. This society is the dynamic factor in tribal life, "the focus and fountainhead of all secular and religious tribal values; it penetrates and dominates all social life as did the medieval Christian Church; it is the *sanctum sanctorum* of the people. Membership in the Poro is prerequisite to entrance into any other secret organization." At the head of the society stands the Grand Master, who must remain invisible to the uninitiated, being invested with the halo of a supernatural being. Since the people believed him to be immortal, his death is kept a secret, his successor being elected in a conclave of prominent Poro men. Popular faith has it that he is able to kill and revive human beings by his magic. Specifically, he is supposed to devour the neophytes and to rebear them at the expiration of their four years' novitiate in a bush "school." If a novice marked with the scarification design characteristic of membership in the Poro succumbs to the effects of the operation, he is said to remain in the Master's belly. The newcomers must eat of a sacred substance, vow silence as to all the proceedings witnessed, and receive a new name that automatically wipes out responsibility for debts incurred or misdeeds committed under the old appellation. Indeed, upon what may be called their graduation, that is to say, their dismissal from the bush, the tyros pretend to have lost all continuity with the past: they fail to recognize their next of kin and pretend to go astray in their natal village. On this occasion there is a solemn procession about the village, the novices walking or crawling past the Grand Master and the King, and the latter strikes a blow on each youth's back. While all members are pledged to mutual aid, a special bond unites those initiated during the same probationary period. The instruction given is partly of a disciplinary, in part of a technical character. The boys learn, above all, to obey their elders, and to bear privation and punishment. But they also get training in athletic exercises, such as climbing and jumping, and they are taught to hunt, to fish, to weave, and to work iron.

It is clear that the Poro is largely a men's tribal organization erecting a rigid barrier not only against women and young tribesmen but against all aliens as well. Moreover, it contains the distinctive features of a *secret* organization, for while all the male villagers must gain entrance, the deeper mysteries are reserved for the older and more prominent men. Further, there are specific forms of training for different strata of society,—the common folk, the soothsayers and magicians, and the sons of the chiefs and nobility. For the last mentioned group vocational education is provided: as prospective councilors they learn all about the tribal traditions, the essentials of the native polity, the rules of succession, and the court ceremonial.

But while the Poro thus reflects existing institutions, it is itself one of the main influences moulding the social structure and political relations. It is in the Poro bush that all important affairs of public life are debated and settled; and new ordinances are announced in the name of the organization. Though the King is theoretically privy to all its activities and is sometimes referred to as its real head, the Grand Master appears as a dangerous rival even in normal times and seriously curtails the royal power during the four years' probation, assuming a large part of the administrative powers otherwise lodged in the sovereign, maintaining bridges and roads, summoning councils, and generally controlling the population. To these national functions connected with the Poro must be added international ones: during the probationary period no wars are tolerated, and even litigation within the tribe is outlawed.

The Sande, which embraces virtually all women, represents a feminine counterpart to the Poro.   Men are as rigorously excluded from the Sande as women from the Poro.   Girls are taken in at from seven to twelve years of age, remain for three years, are scarified and otherwise mutilated, receive new names, and are pledged to secrecy.   There is instruction in the domestic arts, in dancing, and in sex hygiene. A Headwoman serves as the equivalent of the Grand Master; she is shrouded in cloths and masked when appearing in public, and is believed to have supernatural power to convey fertility to human beings. The Sande training period also culminates in a final parade and presentation to the King.

Three other organizations are of more restricted membership and geographical distribution—the Snake, Antelope Horn, and Gbo societies.   The people at large regard them with awe and at times make use of them, but without the sense of profound attachment characteristic of their sentiment for the two tribal associations.

The main purpose of the Snake society is the magical treatment and prevention of snake bites.   The headmen are members by virtue of an hereditary connection with a serpent, others supply the lack of such a relationship by an initiation ceremony at which they demonstrate their fitness by the fearless handling of snakes.

The Antelope Horn organization consists of magicians whose main function it is to determine the sorcerers guilty of mysterious deaths or other occurrences detrimental to the community, and to exorcise the demons possessing them. The society is most intimately related to the Poro and may be defined as a religious police organ of the state. Its name is derived from the horn container of their magical substances.

The Gbo is likewise intimately connected with the Poro and its headman is endowed with the power of transforming himself into the Grand Master or at least of simulating his appearance. Entrance is by means of an initiation fee, and the novice receives as much instruction as seems proper to the three leaders of the organization. The supernatural powers of the society provide an antidote against poison and any form of sorcery. Like the aforementioned societies, the Gbo members arrange public processions; they demonstrate their powers by defiantly devouring rice bewitched *ad hoc* by any of the other tribesmen.

The Leopard society, which is widely distributed in Sierra Leone as well as in Liberia bears a distinctive character. It conforms to the customary pattern of a magical fraternity in having a set of supernatural objects kept in a special receptacle. When this fetish is believed to demand a bloody sacrifice, an assembly is summoned lest evil befall the tribe. A victim is chosen, and the executioner appointed dons a leopard skin that forms part of the sacred outfit and ties iron or wooden talons to his hands before attacking his prey. The murdered person's blood is allowed to drip on the fetish, while his body is dissected and the flesh eaten, the hair or nails being kept for magical purposes.

Though in some localities the Leopard society has gained tremendous influence by luring chiefs and dignitaries of the Poro into its fold, thereby virtually securing political control, the excesses committed not infrequently led to a violent reaction; the people revolted against its tyranny and some chiefs were driven into punishing membership with the death penalty. In fairness it must be said, however, that while the uninitiated stood in terror of the association, its officers often acted from a sense of responsibility for the common weal, which feeding of the fetish was supposed to promote.

If we now try to define briefly the functional value of the several associations, it is obvious that the two tribal societies play by far the most significant part in the lives of the people. They, and they alone, affect the life of every single individual in the tribe; membership in the Poro is prerequisite to entrance into the other associations; and in so far as the others, including the Leopard society, gain ascendancy it is only by either acting as agents of the Poro or by se-

curing control over it. This functional primacy is
confirmed by historical considerations. The Poro
is the most ancient of the societies not only according to native tradition, but also on the strength of
the oldest written sources, for O. Dapper's account
(1670) figures it and its female complement in con-
formity with recent observations. Further, the Poro
is almost uniform throughout the region extending
from the Ivory Coast to Portuguese Guinea; while
the general notion of a men's and women's tribal initiation and correlated associational sex dichotomy
has an enormous distribution in Africa, arguing for a
very respectable antiquity.

Let us now inquire what influence the Kpelle associations exert on the Kpelle state. In order to appreciate their effect we must bring them into relation on
the one hand with the social units founded in blood
relationship, on the other with the principle of royal
sovereignty.

Like various other African peoples, the Kpelle combine matrilineal and patrilineal conceptions. An-
ciently the children belonged to the sib of the mother,
whose eldest brother partly educated and supported
them, being entitled to pawn his nephews or nieces,
while their father had no legal right of protest. The
head of the sib determines important matters connected with the sib-mates' lives, such as betrothals,
and furnishes material aid in case of poverty or litiga-

tion. On the other hand, property is largely transmitted from father to son. While the children
take the mother's sib name, they inherit primarily
the *paternal* taboo. This patrilineal group in a way
balances the matrilineal body, for it, too, comprises a
group of kindred obligated to render mutual aid and
incapable of testifying against one another in court.

But, quite consistently with Schurtz's scheme, it
is not in either the maternal or the paternal lineage
that political activity centers. In every village
there is at least one assembly house, rarely if ever
visited by women, but constantly occupied by male
villagers.[10] There they can be seen drying their
catch of fish or plaiting mats, swinging in their hammocks and gossiping about the latest news. It is
the place to which strangers are welcomed and invited to barter their goods, where all lawsuits are settled, where every corpse lies in state, and where the
chief invites the men for a convivial evening. This
men's house evidently accomplishes in an informal
manner what the Poro effects through more solemn
processes of initiation; it unites into one group all
the males of the community and establishes a *local* tie
between members of unrelated families. In other
words, the association of men by either method is
an instrumentality which at least paves the way for
coöperative action by a territorial body.

[10] Westermann, *op. cit.*, 54 *seq.*, 86 *seq.*

However, the Kpelle have a quite distinct source of statehood in the principle of royal sovereignty, for nominally the King is supreme arbiter in questions of war and peace, the highest court of appeals, and the owner of both the soil and its occupants. Actually, he is little more than the representative of the popular will as expressed by prominent freemen. Without their consent no important decision is normally rendered, the initiative being taken by the elders of the tribe as frequently as by the supposed ruler. Specifically, it is the Poro that retrenches royal prerogative. Its Grand Master has the right of calling meetings of his own accord, of summoning or excluding the King from such assemblies according to his pleasure, and may inflict penalties, even capital punishment, without consultation of other authorities. As Westermann suggests, the power actually exerted by the King depends on his personality rather than on constitutional privileges.

The relationship of royal and associational influence is, indeed, one of the most interesting phenomena of West African ethnography, generally. Contrary to a widely accepted notion, the negroes are not uniformly given to an autocratic polity. The generalization holds if we merely wish to set off sharply the governmental tendencies of such major areas as Africa, North America, and Polynesia. But it cannot be applied wholesale. As has already been pointed out, the Pangwe have no king lording it over thousands of subjects, but only a petty headman for each separatistic village, who is merely the wealthiest man in the community and cannot even force his villagers to construct an assembly house. The "chief" of course in no sense owns the bodies of the natives, and in contrast to conditions in many other African regions the killing of a man precipitates a blood feud between the sibs of the slayer and the slain.[11]

Now such chiefly impotence is undoubtedly atypical for this continent, but limitation of the ruler's influence by councils and particularly by associational groups is by no means unique. Thus, the Ekoi likewise do not represent a strictly monarchical government. The chief may not be the figurehead represented by his Pangwe colleague, but the main power is vested in the council of old men. The head of the Egbo—the society corresponding to the Poro of the Kpelle—is by far the most powerful man in the town, for the association "usurped practically all functions of government, made trade almost impossible for nonmembers and exercised a deep influence on the religious and mystic side of the nation." The Egbo, for example, punished theft, collected debts on behalf of its membership, and flogged uninitiated people who had offended the organization.[12]

[11] Günter Tessman, *Die Pangwe* (1913), I: 56; II: 89, 262, 228 *seq.*
[12] P. A. Talbot, *In the Shadow of the Bush*, (1912), 42–45, 310; *The Peoples of Southern Nigeria* (1926), III: 606.

Indeed, a survey of West African data suggests two alternative lines of development with all intermediate degrees of power distributed between the chief and the associations. Either the men's societies are the real seat of power, dwarfing the royal influence, or the king may utilize the organization of a secret society for purposes of his own. The former limiting case is illustrated by the Egbo of the Ekoi and probably still better by the Ogboni of Yorubaland. For this association of old men makes a mere puppet of the divine king, controlling society through the Oro, a subordinate corporation whose members execute their orders.[13]

But a very different picture is presented by the Kuyu, a tribe living on a tributary of the Likomala, itself an affluent of the Congo. Here there are two outstanding men's associations, the Ottoté and the Panther society. The former seems to correspond more or less to the Poro and other African tribal organizations except that tyros are initiated at a comparatively advanced age, being at least thirty. They have to pay an entrance fee of 200 francs, half of which is kept by the chief. Initiation is scheduled for a month of the year when according to popular belief spirits haunt the bush, so that women are not allowed to approach. *"Ce mois semble avoir été choisi pour mieux écarter les femmes du lieu d'ini-*

[13] Talbot, *ibid.*,758 *seq.* L. Frobenius,*Und Afrika Sprach* (1913), I: 172 *seq.*

tiation.'' However, the most significant phenomenon is the dominant part played in the proceedings
by the chief. It is he that conducts the ceremony, bestows on the candidate the badge of membership, impresses moral instruction on the novice,
and formally introduces him to two sacred effigies
which by ventriloquism are made to speak. They
represent the chief's deceased parents and would
kill a member divulging the secrets of the association.

Still more firmly is the chief's influence strengthened by the Panther cult. An intimate mystic
bond unites a chief with a particular panther, to
slay which would be equivalent to murdering the
ruler himself. A chief who wishes to punish a
tardy debtor spots his face and body panther
fashion, and in this guise steals the offender's goats
or perchance even kills him. The Panther fraternity is very exclusive: of 1,500 males living in two
Kuyu villages only 19 were found to belong to
the organization. Again, it is the chief that initiates, that acts as the sole guardian of the big drum
and as the head priest officiating in the rites. Six additional priests have drums of their own, but all
the officers must be relatives of the chief, who
is thus in complete control and dominates the tribe
by means of his twofold associational connections.[14]

[14] M. A. Poupon, *Étude ethnographigue de la Tribe Kouyou,* in *L'An-thropologie* (1918-19), XXIX: 53-88, 397-435.

To sum up. If the state is characterized by "the maintenance of political order within fixed territorial limits", then the associations uniting *all* members of an area evidently prepare the way for the political integration of that area, while associations of more limited scope are proportionately less effective in that regard,—except in so far as they may be special instruments of the former. Hence it is the men's house and the Poro, not societies like the Snake organization, that have state building efficacy among the Kpelle. However, in so far as the Antelope Horn organization is a special organ of the Poro it is certainly not a factor militating against tribal unity and may even promote it by fulfilling specific needs of the tribal fraternity.

Nevertheless, one unifying force may run counter to another. An obvious short cut to complete integration is autocracy. Where monarchical power is absolute, political order is *ipso facto* established within the area of royal dominion. It is not a mere accident that on African soil, where absolutism so frequently thrives, the blood feud is correspondingly rare,—that it occurs precisely where, as among the Pangwe, there is little central government, while in the southeastern Bantu monarchies the subjects are conceived as the king's property, so that any injury to the person of an individual is no longer a civil offense against the victim or his kin but a crime against the Crown, which alone may claim an indemnity. Where monarchy and a tribal association coexist, the question is whether they become rival forces or join hands, and it is obviously the latter alternative that yields the more elegant solution of the practical problem of statehood.

PLAINS INDIANS

Among the twenty odd North American tribes usually classed as belonging to the Plains area the concentration of authority in a single hereditary ruler, which so commonly figures in Africa, was probably altogether lacking. As Mr. Maurice Greer Smith has shown in a valuable monograph,[15] the council of elders or great warriors was supreme, the head chief being hardly more than a *primus inter pares*. Among the Hidatsa, for example, this official would receive credit when buffalo were abundant or the enemy suffered losses; but he was also held accountable if things went wrong, so that at times there was reluctance to assume the responsibilities of the position. In this region, accordingly, the unifying effect of the associations must be balanced against those of the council rather than of the chief.

Of associations the Plains Indians had, indeed,

---

[15] *Political Organization of the Plains Indians, with Special Reference to the Council,* in *Univ. Studies, Univ. of Nebraska* (1924), XXIV: 1-84.

a goodly variety, both as regards mode of entrance and function. Thus, a century ago the Crow of eastern Montana, who in this respect were very moderate as compared with some of their neighbors, had eight clubs and a considerable series of Tobacco organizations, which may be regarded either as so many chapters of a single religious order or as separate bodies linked together by their common interest in the cultivation of a sacred weed. The clubs, on the other hand, were purely secular, mingling social, military and political functions, while the Tobacco order was strictly ceremonial in character. Admission into the former was free, while the latter could be entered only by a formal initiation that involved heavy payments. To turn to another tribe, the Pawnee of Nebraska elaborated at least three distinct types of association—fraternities of medicine-men; societies deriving authority from the sacred bundles of the tribe; and organizations without official status, but founded on the basis of visions experienced by private tribesmen.

As among the Kpelle, so in the Plains by no means all of the various societies in question had political significance. For example, the Tobacco order was quite devoid of it, especially in its earlier period when it embraced a strictly limited group of people intent on perpetuating the sacred plant. Similarly, the Omaha visionaries who were linked together for joint ceremonial performance because they all happened to have revelations from the buffalo in no sense developed into state-building agencies, and the same applies to the corresponding dream cults of the Dakota.[16] Again, the guilds of proficient tanners and porcupine-quill embroiderers reported from the Cheyenne and Western Dakota, however interesting in themselves, have no bearing on the question of the maintenance of political order within fixed territorial limits.

It is evidently otherwise when we turn to the so-called military societies, but even here some discrimination is imperative. There was a certain individuality about the several tribal schemes, which may be ranged in two categories. With some of the Plains Indians all the societies of this type were on a plane of equality; among the rest they were graded in an hierarchical series, each member of which comprised virtual coevals. We shall find that while in either case there was correlation with governmental activity, the measure of tribal integration that resulted might appreciably differ.

To illustrate the former type, the Crow of Montana, about a hundred years ago, had eight associations, of which the Foxes, Lumpwoods, Dogs, and Bulls remained of some importance for several

[16] Clark Wissler, *Societies and Ceremonial Associations in the Oglala Division of the Teton-Dakota*, in *Anthrop. Pap., Amer. Mus. Nat. Hist.* (1912), XI: 1-99.

decades after their discovery by Prince Maximilian
in 1833. In each there were officers wearing or
carrying distinctive regalia and charged not with
administrative duties but with the honorific obligation never to retreat from the enemy after once
having taken a stand in battle. The election
occurred in the spring, and office was held for a
single year, the actual management of each society's
affairs being in the hands of a nonelective group of
elderly members. Apart from these martial aspects
there was one important political feature common
to all the societies: alternately they assumed the
direction of the people during a communal buffalo
hunt, the chief appointing any one of them to act
as police for one year. Finally, there were the
purely social activities of these organizations, which
met not infrequently in the lodge of a prominent
member to feast and to rehearse their dances and
songs. There was a spirit of mutual helpfulness, so
that the purchaser of a sacred bundle might rely on
his associates' contributing to the price demanded.
Sometimes fellow members would hunt buffalo for
the benefit of one of their number, and this mutual
benefit idea has been displayed even in recent years
by the modern clubs that consider themselves
descended from the military organizations.[17]

[17] Lowie, *Societies of the Crow, Hidatsa and Mandan Indians*, in
Anthrop. Papers, Amer. Mus. Nat. Hist. (1913), XI: 147–217.

Now in what way has this scheme of associations a bearing on the creation of a state? Evidently by no means all of their activities even indirectly further territorial unification. In fact, such associations may prove quite as disruptive a factor as family or sib ties. As a Yurok or Ifugao community is at times rent asunder by the hostilities of family groups within the same locality, so a Plains Indian camp sometimes suffered from the antagonisms of different clubs. Among the Crow, for example, two of the eight associations recorded by Maximilian, the Foxes and the Lumpwoods, grew in numbers to a disproportionate degree in the decades subsequent to his visit and developed an intense spirit of rivalry. This was revealed in two ways: in war and in love. Each of the two organizations sought to surpass the other in deeds of valor. If a Fox had struck the first blow of the year against an enemy, the Lumpwoods were derided and lost the privilege of singing their own songs during that season; and vice versa. Moreover, during a brief period in the spring a Fox was licensed to kidnap the wife of a Lumpwood provided she had previously been his sweetheart, while the Lumpwoods engaged in corresponding abduction of the Foxes' wives.

It is true that this feeling of rivalry is said to have been "quite free from any personal hostility." Undoubtedly that was the *ideal* more or less con-

sciously held up before the membership. There
were certain rules in the code of rivalry and if the
game was fairly played, the other side had no legit-
imate grievance or means of redress. A husband
who offered resistance to a duly qualified kidnapper
lost prestige and became the butt of satirical songs,
especially if he subsequently took back his wife.
Yet when we read the narratives of actual occurrences of this order, a different state of affairs is
revealed. We see that conflict of practice and
theory, that revolt of a natural psychological response against a traditionally imposed norm which
Dr. Malinowski has so vividly pictured for us in his
Crime and Custom in Savage Society (1926). The
loss of a congenial mate, whether legally subject to
capture or not, sometimes elicited intense resent-
ment, which was enhanced by the public displayal
of the captive. To quote a solitary instance, re-
counted by the wife of a distinguished Fox:

"I heard the Lumpwoods outside. They had
taken the wife of a man who had been living with
her peacefully for several years. He got furious and
was going to kill her with an arrow as she was being
shown off. He let fly and barely missed her. The
Lumpwoods all scattered. They took revenge on
the Foxes by cutting up their robes into strips and
pounding their horses' feet."

In the present case untoward developments were

nipped in the bud by the arrival of a messenger announcing that two Crow war parties had been destroyed by the enemy, so that the whole camp went into mourning, but the disruptive potentialities of the kidnapping procedure are obvious.

Similar dangers were always lurking in the rivalry exhibited on the battlefield. No Crow enjoyed being publicly twitted with cowardice, as happened to the whole of either society that failed to score the first blow, and the constant chanting of songs in defiance and mockery of the defeated group hardly made for perfect harmony. Furthermore, in the heat of battle it was not always easy to determine who actually executed the first *coup*, and in one case on record a dispute between two claimants of whom one was a Fox and the other a Lumpwood was averted only through the close relationship of the two warriors, the elder kinsman waiving his claim against the protests of his fellow-Lumpwoods.

This centrifugal tendency inherent in the system is further attested by the naïve testimony of Beckwourth, an early observer, who some time in the twenties of the last century described a feud that had broken out between the Foxes and the Dogs, evidently the predecessors of the Lumpwoods as rivals of the other organization. "The quarrel originated about the prowess of the respective parties. . . ." [18]

[18] Lowie, *ibid.*, 182.

These Crow phenomena are by no means unique.
They are duplicated to an amazing extent among
the Iowa, whose Tukala and Mawatani societies
vied with each other as to bravery and wife steal-
ing. The latter practice was deprecated by the
officers for reasons obvious from Skinner's account.
"If the woman stolen by a Tukala or Mawatani
was the wife of a very prominent and popular man,
the braves might go directly over and take her away
from her abductor and restore her to her husband,
who himself appears to have pretended to be un-
moved by the loss. The braves also made him
gifts to overlook the theft. The thief durst not
keep her for fear of the vengeance of the soldiers,
who might beat or even kill him if he resisted. Or-
dinarily, however, it was the part of the thief's parents to make good the loss of the bereaved husband
by presents." [19] The same features occurred among
the Oglala Dakota, where rivalry between the societies is described as intense. [20]

In short, if these associations succeed in over-
coming the separatism of kin groups by bringing
together men of different families and sibs, they
are quite as capable of dividing the community
along associational lines, and additional factors
are required to establish the territorial bond.

[19] A. B. Skinner, *ibid.*, 697–699.
[20] Wissler, *ibid.*, 74.

Associational particularism can evidently be overcome if the several organizations are subject to
the control of a single authority. That end was
actually achieved even among the Crow, but it
was achieved intermittently, not as a permanent
feature of their communal life, through a most
rigorous surveillance of the camp by whatever society was delegated by the chief to act in that
capacity. Thus, to take a special example: "If
any individual made a premature move so as to
scare the game, the Big Dogs gathered together
and went after him. They addressed him as if talk-
ing to a dog, saying, 'Stop, go back!' The offender
then halted. Next they asked him gently, 'Why
are you moving away?' If the man gave a gentle
reply and obeyed orders, everything was well, but
if he answered in angry tones the Big Dogs whipped
him, sometimes so hard that he could not move."

We have here one of the most characteristic and
widespread phenomena in the culture of the entire
area. Under the grim pressure of economic necessity, the Plains Indians evolved the notion of temporarily suspending that virtually complete free-
dom from coercion usually enjoyed by tribesmen.
As early as 1680 Hennepin reports a telling experience. He had met a party of Santee, who liberally
offered him buffalo meat, when a group of armed
"Savages" swooped down upon the lodge, knocked

it down and confiscated the food. "One of them
. . . told me that those who had given us vict-
uals had done basely to go and forestal the others
in the Chase; and that according to the Laws and
Customs of their Country 'twas lawful for them
to plunder them, since they had been the cause
that the Bulls were all run away, before the Nation
could get together, which was a great Injury to the
Publick . . ."

With amazing uniformity as to detail the police
functions just described have been recorded for a
dozen and more tribes and for a period of two hundred years. The personnel of the constabulary
varies with the tribe; the duties may be linked with
a particular society (Mandan, Hidatsa), or be assumed by various military societies in turn (Crow),
or fall to the lot of distinguished men without reference to associational affiliations (Kansas). But
everywhere the basic idea is that during the hunt a
group is vested with the power forcibly to prevent
premature attacks on the herd and to punish of-
fenders by corporal punishment, by confiscation of
the game illegally secured, by destruction of their
property generally, and in extreme cases by killing
them.[21]

In order to appreciate this phenomenon we must
contrast it with the normal state of affairs among

[21] *Anthrop. Papers, Amer. Mus. Nat. Hist.*, XI: 130, 180, 747, *passim.*

Plains Indian peoples, where the individual, generally speaking, was wholly free from interference in his movements and activities, where nothing was more remote from native conceptions than that a chief should wield power over the property and life of the population. Further, the idea of the family or sib was undoubtedly of tremendous importance in native law. If, for example, a man had been murdered by another, the official peacemakers of the tribe—often identical with the buffalo police—were primarily concerned with pacifying the victim's kin rather than with meting out just punishment. There was thus a groping sentiment on behalf of territorial cohesion and against internecine strife. But there was no feeling that any impartial authority seated above the parties to the feud had been outraged and demanded penance or penalty. In juridical terminology, even homicide was a tort, not a crime. But with transgressions of the hunting regulations it was otherwise: they were treated as an attempt against the public, in short as a criminal act, and they were punished with all the rigor appropriate to political offenses. In other words, for the brief period of the hunt the unchallenged supremacy of the police unified the entire population and created a state "towering immeasurably above single individuals," but which disappeared again as rapidly as it had come into being.

No other feature of Plains Indian life approached the buffalo police as an effective territorial unifier. But in less spectacular fashion a similar result was achieved when the military societies, instead of being coördinate as among the Crow, were serially arranged according to the alternative plan suggested above (p. 96), by which one group of age mates successively bought membership privileges from older groups, the transaction being an outright purchase divesting the older company of their ownership rights. Such an arrangement obviously was not favorable to the separatistic rivalry current among the Crow and Dakota, for since it was a matter of pride to acquire the prerogatives of the higher group, the young men were dependent on their seniors' good will. The negotiation was conceived as a transfer of ceremonial rights to which the fortunate owners would consent only after much cajolery. There was, to be sure, a farcical attempt on the part of the sellers to extort the maximum compensation, while the purchasers were equally bent on paying as little as possible. This haggling was, however, merely part of the game. In connection with this feature of the proceedings there was an alignment of alternate groups, so that "odds" and "evens" were pitted against each other. But this also did not imply a cleavage of the males in the community; it meant no more than an obligation to assist one another in the collective purchases of membership privileges.

As a matter of fact, the scheme involved a positive tendency toward unification. Compared with, say, the grades in some Melanesian club houses, the Plains Indian associations appear as so many mutually independent corporations, each with a sharply defined individuality that found outward expression in separate lodges and distinctive insignia.

Yet in a way these societies seem to be subdivisions of a single order, and it is suggestive of aboriginal sentiment that the Blackfoot designated the whole set jointly as the "All Comrades." Intensive consideration of all the relevant phenomena indicates that the military associations of the graded no less than of the coördinate type, were at one time autonomous units, which were subsequently linked together and more or less accidentally assumed such and such positions in the scale. Accordingly, the arrangement presupposed some measure of integration. The maximum was probably achieved by the Arapaho (originally in Colorado and Wyoming), for here the entire system was under the control of seven men constituting the foremost of the organizations:

"These seven old men embodied everything that was most sacred in Arapaho life. They directed all the lodges. The actual part they played in these consisted chiefly of directing . . . , often only by gestures. . . . Every dance, every song, and every action of the lodges was performed at the direction of these old men." [22]

In this arrangement, however, it is not the occurrence of grades that is essential, but the centralization of responsibility and power. The Skidi Pawnee effected similar smoothness in the working of their military organizations by a quite distinct technique. Their thirteen villages were united under the authority of as many sacred bundles, of which the one linked with the Evening Star was supreme; and all the societies with public functions discharged them under the sanction of these ritualistic aggregations of objects.

SUMMARY

In my book on *Primitive Society* [23] I attached great importance to associations as "potential agencies for the creation of a state by uniting the population within a circumscribed area into an aggregate that functions as a definite unit irrespective of any other social affiliations of the inhabitants." Still more emphatically I wrote in an article on "The Origin of the State" [24] that "associations invariably weaken the prepotency of blood

[22] Kroeber, *The Arapaho*, in *Bull. Amer. Mus. Nat. Hist.* (1902–1907), XVIII: 207 *f.*
[23] 394–396.
[24] *The Freeman* (July, 19 and 26, 1922), V: 440–442, 465–467.

108   THE ORIGIN OF THE STATE

ties by establishing novel ties regardless of kinship; and they may indirectly establish a positive union of all the occupants of a given area. They are thus one of the greatest agencies for strengthening the principle of local contiguity."

Further study leads to serious modification of this view. Undoubtedly the claims set forth for the destructive efficacy of associations hold: by the very fact of their existence they have created novel bonds bound to encroach upon the omnipotence of kinship ties. But their positive achievement is more doubtful: it is only when supplementary factors of unification supervene that they achieve the solidarity of the entire local group. In itself, in other words, associational activity is not less separatistic than the segmentation of society into groups of kindred.

Over-simplification has sometimes obscured this fact. For example, to revert to the Masai, it is customary to describe their division of all males into three groups,—the boys, the initiated bachelors, and the married men. Objectively, these undoubtedly correspond to the three status grades recognized by the tribe. But are we therefore warranted in treating them as so many social units? By no means. It is only the bachelors that cohere as a definitely organized aggregate of individuals. The boys and the "elders" are artificial constructs created by negative definition: they include, respectively, those who are not yet and those who are no longer in the warriors' encampment. Specifically, all those in the elders' grade *might* form a dynamic unit in Masai life, but as a matter of fact they do not. They are split into an indefinite number of age classes, each formed by the men initiated during the same quadrennium. Since the ritual of initiation took place approximately at puberty and since between successive initiation quadrennia there always intervened a period of three and a half years, there were probably at any one time as many as eight or more distinct age classes instead of the three naïvely assumed to correspond to the status grades.

These minor bodies were genuine social units because the mere fact of joint entrance into the warriors' grade created a permanent bond with well defined mutual rights and obligations. While the Masai are divided into exogamous patrilineal sibs, their age classes figure quite as prominently in marital arrangements, though in an endogamous sense. Though a man may mate with a woman of his own "age" (the women being in a series of strata parallel to the men's) and though widows or divorcées are allowed to consort without reproach with their deceased or separated husbands' fellow initiates, no man may have intercourse with a woman of his father's age class. A Masai coming to a strange encampment looks for the hut of an age mate and is forthwith entitled to his host's dwelling and his spouse.

It is true that, so far as the evidence goes, these various classes were not normally in conflict; but the very fact of their occurrence certainly did not make for tribal cohesion, however it may have been compensated for by other factors in tribal life.[25]

That associational activity alone does not suffice to weld people into a national whole is well exemplified by the case of the Chinese. Here there is a mania for organization. There are coöperative loan societies and trade unions, merchant guilds, associations for hunting hares and visiting the sick. People assemble for pilgrimages to sacred mountains or at least simulate a journey and arrange a theater party. In the larger cities the very beggars formally unite to browbeat into almsgiving the participants in a wedding or a funeral procession. Some of these associations undoubtedly assume political functions, as when the peasants of a village jointly maintain sentries to protect their crops against marauders. But this is merely establishing a tie of lesser import—a makeshift for the lacking central protecting agency. Again, there is of course a territorial element in the metropolitan fraternities that embrace all the

[25] M. Merker *Die Masai* (1904) 47 f., 72. A. C. Hollis, *The Masai* (1905), 291, 303, 262 f., 312, 288.

men coming from the same province; but this type of association clearly does not create the local tie, it merely follows in its wake. As we showed in the chapter on Sovereignty, a trade union may oppose the central authority, successfully cope with its agents, and in so far forth nullify national unity.

In short, associations are not inherently either centralizing or disruptive agencies. Everything depends on the correlated factors of integration.

This conclusion is supported by certain interesting facts of geographical distribution. If there were a simple causal connection between associations and territorial integration, political unification should be weak wherever associations are lacking or weakly developed. But the data patently contradict the assumed correlation. It is true that such peoples as the Basin Shoshoneans are at once devoid of societies and centralized government. But, as Schurtz himself did not fail to note, associational activity is rare or absent among the pastoral nomads of Asia, who must be credited with founding some of the most extensive and most closely knit kingdoms of historical times. Obviously, then, associations do not play the preponderant role in political development which I was at one time inclined to ascribe to them.

VI

CONCLUSION

We set out with the intention of vindicating the principle of continuity in the sphere of political history. Before examining to what extent it has proved to hold, it may be well to dispel possible misunderstandings. Modern ethnology rejects the notion of unilinear evolution; it does not, in other words, believe that some mystic *vis politica* urges all societies alike to traverse the same stages towards a strongly centralized state. Hence, it is not possible to grade peoples according to the degree in which they approach that goal; if several distinct paths are conceivable, progress along any two of them becomes incommensurable. China, as described by Giles, is further from the ideal of Bismarck, Roosevelt, or Mussolini than, say, Imperial Germany; she comes nearer to the terminus envisaged by Duguit.

When, therefore, we speak of bridging the chasm between a tiny Andamanese settlement and the British Empire, we deprecate the attempt to indicate the various stages by which the simpler would have necessarily tended to approach the latter. What we have tried to do is simply to prove that the germs

112

of all possible political development are latent but demonstrable in the ruder cultures and that a specific turn in communal experience—say, contact with a weaker or stronger neighbor—may produce an efflorescence of novel institutions.

Specifically, the problem was to determine whether "savage" society recognizes the territorial tie or whether political order is maintained solely on the basis of personal relations, as Maine and Morgan contended. Let us summarize and supplement the discussion in Chapter IV.

It is natural that earlier observers and theorists should have been impressed with the *differences* between primitive and civilized government. The general absence of orderly processes of law—outside of Africa—was sufficient to suggest complete diversity of plan, and on the positive side there was the obvious stress on kinship as a political factor. What the older writers overlooked was the subtler texture of the territorial bond in ancient law, which of course in essence was not different from the generally accepted ethical postulates underlying our own legal institutions as their ultimate sanction and guaranteeing their smooth functioning. It is easy to see that when a Plains Indian kills a fellow tribesman the offense is settled by the kins involved, without recourse to the formalities of a trial by a duly constituted court. But the important point is that the culprit's family acknowledge responsibility and offer compensation: they do not, in short, regard the case as on a par with the slaying of an alien. Even the Ifugao were found to recognize the distinction between fellow resident and outsider in the case of theft and thus completely demolish the theory that coresident kin groups are in their mutual relations the equivalents of so many autonomous states. The argument is of course strengthened when we discover a conventional machinery, purely private among the Ifugao, public (though generally without absolute authority) among the Plains tribes, for adjusting the difficulty in the interests of neighbors not directly involved in the quarrel.

In the book cited above, Dr. Malinowski rightly insists on the *positive* side of primitive law: without the general acceptance of a system of reciprocal services, he argues, communal living would hardly be possible. Nevertheless, for our purpose, it suffices to point to the spectacular reaction of the "collective mind" whenever public opinion is openly flouted: the universal recognition of some deeds as crimes—though the definition of the offenses may vary from tribe to tribe—is a decisive proof of the omnipresence of the state. It is not a crime for an Australian to maim his wife, but it is a crime, formerly punishable with death, to marry within the forbidden degrees of relationship. So a Plains Indian may not be liable for abduction of a married woman, but he is beaten and deprived of his possessions if he disobeys the police during a tribal hunt.[1] However, it is not difficult to find instances of local integration within the domain of *civil* law, provided we admit that the political sphere may be otherwise defined than in Western civilization. With us, for instance, confirmation is a private matter, concerning only the family in question; in many primitive societies, public activity may almost be said to center in the more or less equivalent adolescence rites. Their proper performance is among the most serious problems confronting an aboriginal council in Australia,—quite apart from the serious crime committed by an initiate who should divulge the secrets of admission. Similarly, in the more loosely organized Andamanese settlement, the corresponding ceremonies for both sexes are matters engaging the attention of the headman, who personally anoints a novice with honey in order to free him from the dietary taboo on that delicacy.

That local contiguity is a real basis for union on primitive levels may thus be taken as an established fact. It cannot be said that we have been equally successful in demonstrating the agencies for intensifying this element; for associational

[1] Lowie *Primitive Society*, 406 seq.

activity, on which we formerly leaned heavily, lends only partial aid. For supplementary assistance we must have recourse to that principle of Sovereignty which in an earlier chapter received but scant recognition. But while it cannot be taken as an essential of statehood, it has genuine value as a limiting concept. In other words, we can gauge the importance of the territorial factor by the measure of sovereignty extant. The Pangwe, who permit a blood feud to rage when a tribesman is killed, less uniformly maintain public order within fixed territorial limits than the Southeastern Bantu, among whom homicide, as well as assault and battery, is never a tort against the sufferer and his family but a crime against the king, who alone is entitled to an indemnity. Joint submission to the ruling monarch evidently is the means by which territorial unification is secured.

Though permanent concentration of power in a single person's hands is thus the simplest way to impose the territorial bond, it is not the only one. The meteoric display of sovereign authority by the Plains Indian buffalo police shows how an almost anarchic community may be rapidly, if only temporarily, placed under martial law. A coercive force, then, whether vested in a person or a group seems the short cut to intensifying and bringing into consciousness the incipient feeling of neighborliness that has been found a universal trait of human society. Once established and sanctified, the sentiment may well flourish without compulsion, glorified as loyalty to a sovereign king or to a national flag.